World Wisdom
The Library of Perennial Philosophy

The Library of Perennial Philosophy is dedicated to the exposition of the timeless Truth underlying the diverse religions. This Truth, often referred to as the *Sophia Perennis*—or Perennial Wisdom—finds its expression in the revealed Scriptures as well as in the writings of the great sages and the artistic creations of the traditional worlds.

World Wheel I-III appears as one of our selections in the Writings of Frithjof Schuon series.

The Writings of Frithjof Schuon

The Writings of Frithjof Schuon form the foundation of our library because he is the preeminent exponent of the Perennial Philosophy. His work illuminates this perspective in both an essential and comprehensive manner like none other.

T0307012

World Wheel

Volumes I-III

Poems by

Frithjof Schuon

Foreword by
Annemarie Schimmel

Introduction by
William Stoddart

Translated from the German

World Wisdom

World Wheel
Volumes I-III
©2006 World Wisdom, Inc.

Library of Congress Cataloging-in-Publication Data

Schuon, Frithjof, 1907-1998.
  [Poems. English. Selections]
  World wheel, volumes I-III : poems / by Frithjof Schuon ; foreword by
Annemarie Schimmel ; introduction by William Stoddart.
    p. cm. -- (Writings of Frithjof Schuon series) (Library of perennial
philosophy)
  "Translated from the German."
  Includes bibliographical references and index.
  ISBN-13: 978-1-933316-25-3 (pbk. : alk. paper)
  ISBN-10: 1-933316-25-X (pbk. : alk. paper) 1. Schuon, Frithjof,
1907-1998--Translations into English. 2. Religious poetry, German--
20th century. I. Schimmel, Annemarie. II. Stoddart, William. III. Title.
  PT2680.U474A2 2006c
  831'.914--dc22

                                                    2006030904

Cover: Frithjof Schuon
Photograph by Whitall Perry

Printed on acid-free paper in Canada

For information address World Wisdom, Inc.
P.O. Box 2682, Bloomington, Indiana 47402-2682

www.worldwisdom.com

Contents

Foreword

It seems that mystical experience almost inevitably leads to poetry. The great mystics all over the world used the language of poetry when trying to beckon to a mystery that lies beyond normal human experience, and the most glorious works in Eastern and Western religions are the hymns of the mystics, be they Sufis or Christians, Hindus or Zen monks. Different as their expressions are, one feels that the poetical word can more easily lead to the mystery that is hidden behind the veils of intellectual knowledge and which cannot be fettered in logical speech.

In the world of Islam, the love-intoxicated poems of Maulana Jalaladdin Rumi are considered by many to be "the Koran in the Persian tongue," and Rumi is only one of many intoxicated souls who expressed their love and longing, and their experience of the Divine Unity, in verse. And even those mystics who preferred a more "intellectual" approach to the Absolute couched their experiences in verse. The prime example is, of course, Ibn Arabi whose *Tarjuman al-ashwaq* translated his experience of the One, Unattainable Deity into the language of traditional Arabic poetry.

Taking this fact into consideration we are not surprised that Frithjof Schuon too felt compelled to write poetry—and, it is important to note, poetry in his German mother tongue. His verse sometimes reflects ideas and images of R. M. Rilke's *Stundenbuch*, in which the expert on mysticism can find some strange echoes of Ibn Arabi's ideas. This may be an accident, for mystical ideas are similar all over the world; but the German reader of Schuon's verses enjoys the familiar sound. This sound could not be maintained in the English translations of his poetry. Yet, as he himself explains, what really matters is the content, and here we listen to the thinker who, far from the intricate and complex scholarly sentences of his learned prose works, sings the simple prayers of the longing soul: God is the center, the primordial ground which comprehends everything, manifesting Himself through the colorful play of His creations. And it is the human heart which alone can reflect the incomprehensible Being, for humanity's central quality is divinely inspired love, which is the axis of our life.

I hope that Schuon's mystical verse will be read not only by English speaking readers but even more by those who understand German.[1] They will enjoy many of these tender lyrics which show the famous thinker in a very different light and from an unexpected side.

—Annemarie Schimmel, Professor Emeritus, Harvard University

---

[1] See Translator's Note on page *xvi*.

Introduction

Frithjof Schuon (1907-1998) was a sage, an artist, and a poet. During the last three years of his life, he wrote in German—his mother tongue— approximately 3,500 short poems, in 23 separate collections. In content, Schuon's German poems are similar to those in his English collection *Road to the Heart*, but they are much more numerous, and the imagery is even more rich and powerful. The poems cover every possible aspect of metaphysical doctrine, spiritual method, spiritual virtue, and the role and function of beauty. They express every conceivable subtlety of spiritual and moral counsel—and this not merely in general terms, but with uncanny intimacy, detail, and precision. They exhibit incredible sharpness, profundity, comprehensiveness, and compassion. They are his final gift to the world, his testament and his legacy.

Some of the poems are autobiographical, with reminiscences of places experienced: Basle and Paris, the fairy-tale streets of old German towns, Morocco and Andalusia, Turkey and Greece, the American West. Others evoke the genius of certain peoples, such as the Hindus, the Japanese, the Arabs, the Red Indians, and also the Cossacks and the Gypsies. Yet other poems elucidate the role of music, dance, and poetry itself. In one or two poems, the godless modern world comes in for biting, and sometimes fiercely humorous, comment:

> *Ein weltlich Fest: Lampenkristalle schimmern*
> *Im großen Saal —*
> *Und glänzende Gesellschaft, Damen, Herrn,*
> *Sitzen beim Mahl.*
> *Man spricht von allem und man spricht von nichts —*
> *Der Wein ist rot,*
> *Und so der Blumenschmuck.*
> *Doch keiner, keiner*
> *Denkt an den Tod.*

A worldly banquet: chandeliers glitter
     In the large hall —
And brilliant society, ladies and gentlemen

Sit down for the meal.
They talk of everything and they talk of nothing —
The wine is red,
And so are the flowers.
But no one, no one
Thinks of death.

(*Stella Maris*, "The Celebration")

The poems embody both severity and compassion. They are powerfully interiorizing. Their content epitomizes Schuon's teaching, which he himself has summarized in the words Truth, Prayer, Virtue, and Beauty. For him, these are the four things needful; they are the very purpose of life, the only source of happiness, and the essential means of salvation. The poems convey these elements to the reader not only mentally, but also, as it were, existentially; their role is both doctrinal and sacramental.

The central role of prayer is powerfully expressed in the following poem entitled "*Panakeia*" ("panacea," the remedy for all ills):

Warum hat Gott die Sprache uns geschenkt?
Für das Gebet.
Weil Gottes Segen dem, der Ihm vertraut,
Ins Herze geht.

Ein Beten ist der allererste Schrei
in diesem Leben.
So ist der letzte Hauch ein Hoffnungswort —
Von Gott gegeben.

Was ist der Stoff, aus dem der Mensch gemacht,
Sein tiefstes Ich?
Es ist das Wort, das uns das Heil gewährt:
Herr, höre mich!

Why has God given us the gift of speech?
For prayer.
Because God's blessing enters the heart of him
Who trusts in God.

The very first cry in this life
Is a prayer.

And the last breath is a word of hope —
      Given by God.

What is the substance of which man is made,
      His deepest I?
It is the Word that grants us salvation:
      Lord, hear me!

         (*Stella Maris*, "Panacea")

Many of the poems express the purpose of life with unmistakable clarity, for example:

Jedes Geschöpf ist da, um "Gott" zu sagen;
So musst auch du der Welt Berufung tragen,
O Mensch, der du der Erde König bist —
Weh dem, der seines Daseins Kern vergisst;

Dies tut nicht Tier noch Pflanze, ja kein Stein;
Dies tut der willensfreie Mensch allein
In seinem Wahn.
        Sprich "Gott" in deinem Wandern;
Es werde eine Gnade für die Andern.

Denn eine Aura strahlt vom Höchsten Namen —
Gebet ist Segen, ist der Gottheit Samen.

All creatures exist in order to say "God";
So must thou too accept the world's vocation,
O man, who art king of the earth —
Woe unto him who forgets the kernel of his existence;

No animal, no plant nor stone does this;
But only man, with his free will,
In his madness.
        Say "God" throughout thy life;
It will be a grace for others too.

For an aura radiates from the Supreme Name —
Prayer is blessing; it is the seed of the Divine.

         (*Stella Maris*, "The Aura")

But the dread consequences of a wrong choice are not forgotten:

> *In Indien sagt man oft, dass Japa-Yoga*
> *Stets Segen bringe — dass das Rāma-Mantra*
> *Ein Wundermittel sei, das helfen müsse.*
> *Dem ist nicht so, denn zürnen kann Shrī Rāma.*

> In India it is often said that *Japa-Yoga*
> Always brings blessings — that the *Rāma-Mantra*
> Is a miraculous means, that cannot but help.
> This is not so, for Shrī Rāma can also show His wrath.
>
> (Songs without Names I-XXXIII)

> *Und Gottes Zorn — er war zuvor schon da;*
> *Denn Gottes Nein begleitet Gottes Ja.*
> *Ihr fragt: war Gott zuerst nicht reine Milde?*
> *Des Zornes Möglichkeit war auch im Bilde.*

> And God's anger — it was already there;
> For God's No accompanies God's Yes.
> You ask: is God not first and foremost Mercy?
> The possibility of anger is also in the picture.
>
> (Songs without Names II-LXXII)

> *Das Gottgedenken muss den Menschen ändern,*
> *Denn zum Beleuchten gibt die Lampe Licht;*
> *Wenn unsre Seele nicht verbessert wird,*
> *Dann zählt das Sprechen frommer Formeln nicht.*

> *Lass ab von falscher Größe — werde klein*
> *Und selbstlos, und du wirst im Himmel sein.*

> God-remembrance must change man,
> For the purpose of a lamp is to give light;
> If our soul is not improved,
> Then reciting pious formulas is of no avail.

> Renounce false greatness — become small
> And selfless, and thou wilt be in Heaven.
>
> (Songs without Names IV-II)

Our human smallness is exposed without pity:

Lärmendes Nichts ist manche Menschenseel —
Was bläht sie sich, als wär sie gottgeboren?
Ein kurzer Erdentraum voll Eitelkeit,
Ruhloses Tun — und alles ist verloren.

Besinnet euch: seid klein, denn Gott ist groß.
Er hat euch eine Heimat zubereitet
Im Himmelreich: ein goldner Zufluchtsort —
Wohl dem, der gegen seine Seele streitet!

Many a human soul is a noisy void —
Why is she inflated as if born of God?
A brief earthly dream, full of vanity,
Restless activity — and all is lost.

Remember: be small, for God is great.
He has prepared for you a homeland
In the Kingdom of Heaven, a golden shelter —
Blessèd is he who fights against his soul!

(*Adastra,* "Smallness")

Again and again, the poems return to the perplexing and agonizing problem of evil:

Da wo das Lichte erscheinet,
    Da muss auch das Finstere drohen;
Wundre und gräme dich nicht;
    So will es das wirkende Sein.
Siehe, die niederen Mächte
    Bekämpfen heimtückisch die hohen;
Da wo ein Abel erstrahlet,
    Da ist auch ein finsterer Kain.

Denn die Allmöglichkeit Gottes
    Erfordert ja auch die Verneinung:
Wahrheit und Friede sind himmlisch,
    Irdisch sind Falschheit und Krieg.
Ohne das Übel der Trennung,
    Wo wäre das Gut der Verneinung?

Ohne der Finsternis Treiben,
   Wo wäre der Trost und der Sieg?

Wherever light appears
   Darkness must also threaten;
Do not wonder and grieve,
   Existence will have it thus.
See how the lower powers
   Maliciously battle the higher;
Wherever Abel shines,
   There also is dark Cain.

For God's All-Possibility
   Also demands negation:
Truth and Peace are of Heaven,
   Earthly are falsehood and war.
Without the evil of separation,
   Where would be the good of reunion?
Without the work of darkness,
   Where would be solace and victory?

                              (*Adastra*, "Cosmos")

   No translation can possibly do full justice to the "poetry"—the meter, rhyme, verbal appositeness, allusions, music, inspiration—of the original German. Each German poem is a diamond—sparkling and clear, an architectural masterpiece full of light.

   In his rich profusion of references to the many and varied cultural forms of Europe and beyond—the streets of the Latin Quarter, Andalusian nights, the Virgen del Pilar, the Macarena, sages such as Dante, Shankara, Pythagoras and Plato, the Psalms of David, Arab wisdom, the graces of the Bodhisattvas, Tibetan prayer-wheels, Samurai and Shinto, the songs of love and longing of many peoples—in all of these diverse cultures, Schuon captures the timeless message of truth and beauty which each contains, and renders it present in a most joyful way. When these cultural forms happen to be ones that the reader himself has known and loved, the joy that emanates from the poems is great indeed.

   Schuon's long cycle of poems has already been compared to Rumi's *Mathnāwī*. I think that many of his poems can also be compared to the Psalms of David: they are an expression of nostalgia, of mankind's longing for, and ultimate satisfaction in, the Lord. Their main theme is trustful prayer to an ever-merciful God, and benevolence towards men of goodwill. First and foremost, the poems are instruments of instruction. As such, they are a powerful propulsion towards the inward.

A blessing lies not only in the quality of the poems, but also in the quantity—they constitute an all-inclusive totality. On the one hand, Schuon's German poems recapitulate the teachings contained in his philosophical works in French; on the other, they are an inexhaustible, and ever new, purifying fountain—a crystalline and living expression of the *Religio perennis*. They epitomize truth, beauty, and salvation.

—William Stoddart

Translator's Note

Schuon considered his poems didactic in nature and termed them "Sinngedichte," or teaching poems. With this in mind, the aim of the present English edition is to provide a literal rendering of the German text that remains as true as possible to the author's meaning. These translations are the work of William Stoddart, in collaboration with Catherine Schuon and Tamara Pollack. The translations draw extensively on Schuon's own informal, dictated translations. For a full appreciation of the lyrical resonance and musicality of the original, the reader is referred to the several German editions of these poems currently available.[1]

The last nineteen of these twenty-three collections are grouped under two primary headings, *Songs without Names I-XII* and *World Wheel I-VII*. The chronological order in which these collections were written, spanning three years from 1995-1998, is as follows: *Adastra*, *Stella Maris*, *Autumn Leaves*, *The Ring*, *Songs without Names I-V*, *World Wheel I*, *Songs without Names VI-XII*, and *World Wheel II-VII*.

---

[1] The complete German text of these poems is available in ten volumes from Editions Les Sept Flèches, 1062 Sottens, Suisse, www.sept-fleches.com, as a bilingual German/French edition. A complete bilingual German/Spanish edition is in preparation for 2007 from José J. de Olañeta, Editor, Palma de Mallorca, Spain. Selections can also be found in: *Liebe, Leben, Glück*, and *Sinn* (Freiburg im Breisgau: Verlag Herder, 1997); *Songs for a Spiritual Traveler* (Bloomington: World Wisdom, 2002); and *Adastra & Stella Maris: Poems by Frithjof Schuon* (Bloomington: World Wisdom, 2003).

World Wheel

First Collection

I

The world wheel turns, and thou art the center
Because thou carriest the Spirit which contains the universe
And which is divine, without beginning, without end;
Where the point is, there is the whole world.

II

The first thing is
Piously to remember the Real; then, to accept
Whatever happens to thee as coming from God;
And then to know that thy destiny blossoms in God's hands.

III

The inward and the outward.
Creator and Creation, garment of our Lord.
Soul and body; Spirit and Word;
The world-wheel's center and rotation's rim.

Think not that the outward is small and insignificant —
The form must be the expression of its content.

IV

Content, container: the latter is sacred
Through the former. So despise not
What is mere vehicle. Whatever expresses
The Divine is God's Countenance.

The soul should thus become what the Spirit
Has received from God. Everything is Divine
Which manifests God's Nature through its form.

V

What justifies the repetition of things
Already said? Not the new form,
But the deep richness of the Mystery;
Hence the gift of a new accentuation —

The True which shifts its emphasis.
Just as, in a new abode, one loves with the same heart
But in a new way, what one has loved before.

VI

Firstly: Truth is Peace —
This is what every heart must carry within itself.
Secondly: God's wise providence is here —
Thou shouldst trust and shouldst not ask.

VII

"The Lord made women dear to me,"
Mohammed said. Ibn 'Arabi explains:
This is because the whole loves its half;
Because, in loving, wisdom turns to beauty.

As Plato said: "The beautiful is the splendor
Of the true" — the two mysteries have gone hand in hand
Ever since world and life began.

VIII

In India some say that men of genius,
If they are good, are *jivan-muktas* —
"Delivered in this life." One should not take
This literally; but one can easily see
That great creators, such as Beethoven,
In their art often walk with the angels.

IX

I heard it preached that faith
Is unnecessary, if we are good people.
What does one call goodness? If a man boasts,
All his good actions are lost in the wind.

X

Heresy is a shifting concept —
It is heretical to deny what saves us.
Also heretical is a limited viewpoint
That is suitable only for certain souls;
And likewise the opinion that only color is light:
That only one form of faith can be the Truth.

But if one measures with the measure of Truth,
Only Primordial Wisdom is orthodox.

XI

Everything on earth has an end.
When a poem comes, I think it is the last;
Maybe it would be better if, before God,
I replaced it with some other act.

I have often thought I would lay down my pen,
As I have already said everything.
But I am not the Master of my songs;
I cannot withhold God's gift.

Certainly, whatever is useful should reach the world —
And may it be received with an open mind.

XII

Every woman who is beautiful and noble
Brings something of Shrī Lakshmī to this earth —
Something that blesses it; so that the world,
Through Heaven's nearness, becomes purer and better.

XIII

What reminds us of God? Not beauty alone,
But also greatness: majesty, dignity, strength,
And great deeds; greatness bears witness to the Lord,
As do all the wonders the Most High creates —
As does also love, our life's star.

XIV

The basilica in Rome was magnificent.
The Renaissance destroyed this splendor
And replaced it with oppressive ostentation;
It stabbed the Church in the heart,
Unleashed the whole deceit and lie of modern times,
And thus made the whole world sick.

The Renaissance — in German called "neo-Antiquity";
A better expression would be "neo-paganism."

XV

The wooden buildings of Japan. How wonderful is the idea
Of ceaselessly rebuilding the same buildings —
And entrusting the indestructibility of the shrines of the gods
To the priests and the faithful.

XVI

Shrī Rādhā, lonely in Vrindāvan's forest:
"Divine Flute Player, come soon —
I thirst after Heaven's melodies."

For beauty tells us that God has forgiven us.

XVII

Let no one say that man does not need
The beautiful; for all religions
Lived in beauty, while they still bloomed freely —
Something they no longer do in this time of sick epigones;
Rome was falsified from the Cinquecento onwards —
The "greatness" of the art-destroyers was a mania.

In our age of ugliness we more than ever
Need the beautiful in order to live
As men should live.
　　　　　　　　In order to lift the soul
From the din of the world, up to Heaven.

XVIII

The agreeable has two aspects:
One that is harmful, and another that is uplifting;
Mysticism sees only the harmful side;
Gnosis sees that in which Divinity lives.

XIX

God-remembrance — the Prophet said —
Is not only thinking of the Most High;
It is also all noble things that lead the soul
To that remembrance, and to salvation.

XX

Some do what they read in the law;
For others the law is the nature of things.
The pious call good what the Most High loves;
The wise call good what derives from Being.

Not everyone is a penitent in the desert,
Nor a Krishna who kissed the *gopis*.
There are diverse viewpoints in the Spirit's realm —
The paths that God blesses are of equal value.

XXI

Someone asked an Australian aboriginal:
"Why do you shut your ears to what is new,
To our progress, and to our religion?"
He replied: "You ought not to disturb our peace —
What alone counts for us is That which is, and never was not;
It is invisible, and it is wondrous."

XXII

God is not man; thou art not only an I;
The will is not everything, nor is sentiment.
Within thee is the pure Intellect; in it dwells God.
Whoever loves the Truth is in God's Will.

XXIII

God deep in the heart — chatter all around;
Blessèd repose in the midst of human agitation.
The fate of man, and the life of the wise —
Nothing other could destiny weave for thee.

XXIV

A monk from Mount Athos once told me
That only as Trinity is God understandable.
I say: God possesses Trinity; Trinity does not
Possess God; the Most High is infinite.

XXV

Shankaracharya praised that man as blessed
Who, as an ascetic, sings: *Tat Tvam Asi;*
But also the *jivan-mukta*, the delivered one,
When a child or a woman brings him delight;
He mourns with the one who suffers,
And rejoices with him who trembles with love.

Whatever be his joy and suffering —
The freedom of the delivered one dwells in his heart.

XXVI

Beauty of the Void: it sounds like a contradiction,
Yet is understandable; for Heaven's vault
Is beautiful in its silence; as is also the snow
When, as if in blessing, it falls on the land.

And likewise the soul, when it has forgotten
All triviality, because God's fullness has come.

XXVII

To live means to take many burdens upon oneself
But only for a time — a consolation is always there:
There is the Most High, the Immovable —
Even when happiness seems far from you, God is near!

This is the argument, the absolute argument,
That always lies in your hand.
Be content — God is. "I am That I am."
There is nothing truer or better here below.

XXVIII

Pettiness is part of life — it shames
The soul that loves truth, greatness, beauty.
There is no bridge from the petty to the great,
Which alone gives life its meaning.

Thou canst not philosophize away
The noise that is unworthy of life.
Truth's greatness makes existence luminous —
The Real which is here, which awaits thee, and
To which thou belong'st — and which belongs to thy spirit.

XXIX

That we take pleasure in little earthly things
Does not have as consequence that we rejoice in the Spirit;
On the other hand, when we are happy in the Spirit,
This means that God may grant us other joys,

And more besides. The Most High does not bargain,
But readily gives more than one expects —
So that we may consecrate earthly things to Heaven.

XXX

There is a loving that wants to possess —
And another that rejoices in loving,
In the nature of things: in the unborn
Glory of the man or woman friend.

Dante and Petrarch; Beatrice and Laura —
Singing of longing, but with a higher striving,
Under the sign of heavenly contemplativity.

Mysticism of faith, the poems of St. Teresa;
Saint Bernard said: "I love because I love."

XXXI

When something — good or bad — is of importance,
It has an emanation that proclaims it;
If not, then it has no importance —
And nothing to do with fundamental questions.
Where there is a cause, there must also be an effect,
Be this great or small;
It is said that we should call things by their name —
"By their fruits ye shall know them."

XXXII

It is a fact that every religion
Has two dimensions: one that it proclaims,
Idea, Word, or Myth; and one that it possesses,
But does not dare to express outwardly.

And then there is a third: the two are interwoven,
The formal and the supra-formal from Above;
Different psychic worlds, different levels of Truth —

Three spiritual languages that call to the One.

XXXIII

Different spiritual paths. One must know:
In principle one leads farther, higher,
Than the other. But in fact,
God alone knows where He will lead someone;
For He is the Seer of all destiny's goals.

XXXIV

Fall of the titans. It may happen that while striving on the Path,
Someone falls from a height; but know:
This would not be possible without an opening —
The evil one takes advantage of the soul's fissures.
The calamity is great, even if the door is small;
Without humility, the heart cannot be secure.

XXXV

"Brahma is real; the world but appearance;
The human soul is a ray from Brahma."
Thus speaks the Revelation —
The Sophia that I choose.

Love God with all thy strength,
I was told when I was young.
Thou must never forget prayer —
More I did not ask.

XXXVI

"Grandfather, Great Spirit, have pity,
So that I and mine may live."
Such was the prayer of the Lakota warrior —
He wanted Heaven's blessing for his tribe.

This is the nature of prayer: thy praying
Also helps others in their plight.

XXXVII

With the true sage there is always holiness,
But a holy man is not always a sage.
Noble character they have in common;
But different is the spirit's journey.

The saint is rooted in will and love;
The sage, in knowledge and intelligence.
Certainly, the saint also can have wisdom —
There are many paths in the Spirit's land.

XXXVIII

A need for explanation is natural —
Not so curiosity, which is groundless;
Seek not to know what is not worth knowing —
What would not enrich you, if you knew it.

XXXIX

In worship, long-drawn-out-ness
And complication — whether in small things or in great —
Are the fault of pedants. Simplicity
Does not offend the Sacred.
Certainly one must entertain the masses —
But one can also manifest the sacred in a simple way.
Unless richness and length are
Necessary to convey the music of Heaven,
And what one otherwise would rightly criticize,
Lies in the very nature of things.

XL

Man is often tired of himself —
The devil seeks to meddle in his plight.
So know, O man: in God's golden "now"
Thou wilt always be renewed and refreshed.

For the one who remembers the Lord, is chosen —
In each call, thou art born anew.

XLI

Ask me, what is the object?
             It is what distracts us from outside;
Whereas consciousness of God
             dwells within us —
But the Object is first and foremost
             the Highest, Real Being,
Which encompasses the consciousness of living creatures
             within the framework of existence.

Ask, what then is the subject?
             It is groping, fallible thought;
Whereas the outwardly Real
             is what it is and what it must be —
But a priori: the Subject is
             the Deepest, Divine Self,
Which essentially contains
             manifesting, infinite Reality.

XLII

"There is no Highest Reality, if not
The One Real." This means first:
There is only One God, who created you,
To Whom ye pray — your Consolation and Light.

Then it means: apart from the Absolute,
Everything is imprisoned in relativity.
Whatever is not Being, call it nothingness.

Glory belongs to the Great All.

XLIII

Certitude of God, then peace of the soul —
How canst thou, man, despair over earthly matters?
Certitude contains trust, peace brings joy —
And God will carry thy burdens with thee.

XLIV

If thou saw'st a tree bearing fruit
In winter, thou couldst not understand it;
Be not astonished, O man, beyond all measure —
God sees in any case what we see not.

XLV

"Tell me whom thou frequentest, and I will tell thee who thou art."
Frequent people who honor the sacred;
Sat-Sangha — the "company of the pure" —
Will increase the purity of thy soul.

Purity: humility before God and humility before the one
Who speaks in the name of the Most High.
To see things as they truly are —
Whoever overestimates himself, does not please God.

XLVI

"I will do this tomorrow, if God wills" —
In shā'a 'Llāh — so say the Moslems.
Without consciousness of our dependence on God,
The Moslem will undertake nothing.

It is praiseworthy to cast such a glance toward
The Most High — for it is God-remembrance.

XLVII

Outside, by the gate,
I love to be alone,
And listen to the birds
In the late sun's light.

I have lost myself,
No longer know who I am;
For the Great One alone
I bear now in my mind.

Yet many things exist
That are worthy of my love;
God turned my heart to the One
In the image of Himself.

XLVIII

St. Nonnos had to baptize Pelagia —
Naked the beauty entered the pool;
And Nonnos exclaimed: praised be our Creator
Who made what leads some to perdition,
To be for others a sign of God's Kingdom.

XLIX

One asks the question, why is there Existence —
Could there not just as well be emptiness?
What caused Reality to clothe itself
In the appearance of so many things?

Ye may ask me: what is reality? —
What is real, is necessity:
What exists must be, and ask not for the reason —
The Great One wills the play of multiplicity.

L

To see things in God,
To see God in things;
To see things in themselves,
To stand with God above them —

This is the book of the world,
There is no other;
The reader is thy heart —
There is no other light.

LI

The great peace of the soul is not thinking;
It comes from Being, and like it, is absolute;
Ask not how or why — for God is God;
May He give the soul the grace of Peace,

If it opens itself. — Filled with certitude
And without concern, may it rejoice
Within its deepest core in Pure Being.

LII

I knew, very early, the Bhagavad Gita;
And before that, the Psalms and the Sermon on the Mount;
And then the core saying of Islam, the *Shahādah*;
Each came at its proper time and place.

God has sown many seeds for salvation in this world —
Blessèd are those into whose hearts the seed falls.

LIII

A woman from Senegal could hardly pray,
Arabic was too difficult for her. People thought
She was too stupid even for religion;
No wonder people laughed at her.

But one day — who could accompany her?
She was seen singing, walking on the water.

LIV

The murder of Hypatia: the hatred blind faith bears
For gnosis, the wine of knowledge;
Did not Christ himself say to the people:
"Let him who is without sin cast the first stone."

LV

One wants to pull the mote out of one's brother's eye,
But in one's own eye one does not see the beam.
Thus it is when they flourish in stupid pride,
As if the Most High's Judgement did not exist.

Only he who knows himself thoroughly
Has the right to give counsel to his neighbor;
Only he who has burnt his own illusion,
Can strive with good conscience towards the Most High.

LVI

Everyone carries the saint deep in himself,
And with it the Spirit's luminous primordial powers.
However, one forsakes one's better self —
And thus the saint can never unfold.

In the first case, O man, God was thy Creator;
For thy renewed self thou art the potter.

LVII

To understand metaphysical theories
Is not yet wisdom; and it will be of no avail
If those who have read about them
Walk not the paths of true wisdom,
However much they seek to rely on their literal expression.

Be noble in thy dealings with noble things —
Thou canst not obtain by force the fruits of the spirit.
Many a fool who lifted a veil
Deceived and poisoned his soul —
Think of the cymbals that tinkle without love.

LVIII

Thou askest what is Being. Being is possibility —
Were there no possibility, there would be no Being.
Being or nothingness; which does Reality wish?
That which is not nothing, is Infinity.

The Real wished to give Itself —
It wished to give existence even to nothingness.

LIX

I praise the eagle and the swan,
Lightning from Heaven and peace on the pond;
By night, the owl, in early morn, the cock —
The Creator has given us rich teachings here below.
The peacock and the pheasant — blue-green splendor
And gold, God's fairy art has made;
The little song birds — see what a world
The Lord unfolds beneath the vault of Heaven;
I mention the lark and the nightingale —
In field and wood thou hearest their sweet song.

Heaven saw that I did not feel well —
In the book of nature it allowed me to read.

LX

Certainly, the great spiritual arguments —
Against an evil that weighs down the soul —
Are swiftly victorious; yet when destiny's sting
Is fresh, God's Mercy is worth the grief.

The arguments: the perfection of Being;
And God's goodness, and Eternity.

Saints too have ridden into battle;
Think not that prophets never had to suffer.

LXI

In Rome, Christians were severely persecuted;
Yet: the Romans were not intolerant;
Only because the Christians threatened the Roman world,
Were they dragged without pity before the court.

In the Christian realm Plato's world was crushed;
So one scarcely has the right to complain.

LXII

Japanese music — the melancholy sounds
Of strings flow from the koto like tears;
Ephemerality — the deep meaning of the song;
A butterfly's dream in tender tones.

Beyond the dreaming: here is the wild warrior,
And there the monk, victorious over existence.

LXIII

Human nature wishes to be happy—
And likewise: it must strive towards the Truth,
For otherwise it is not human.
Happiness must flow from the highest Truth.

LXIV

Out in the forest,
The nightingale sings;
It sings of many beauties,
It praises the divine All.

It sings of the lovely flowers
That God strew on the meadows;
And of the twinkling stars,
That are beyond our time.

The flowers wither away,
They are not like the stars.
But they will not perish
In God's eternal Kingdom.

LXV

They think of God and count
Their prayers in the flickering light;
With devotion they turn their holy beads,
Until the thread breaks.

High above a lark is singing,
Full of joy before God's Face;
It trills as it rises in the sky,
And counts not its jubilations.

Did not St. Bernard say:
Love is, because it is love?
And blessèd he who out of love,
Forgets counting — and forgets himself.

LXVI

Prayers with a rosary:
I do not criticize the counting;
But I love the jubilant lark
That counts not when speaking to God.

Each thing in its place:
Strict forms there must be.
With oft-repeated words
Thou canst sow graces in existence.

Ye think that with prayer-wheels
One can liberate nothing;
Yet one can consecrate one's soul
To pious love of one's neighbor.

LXVII

Essential and non-essential; a fool is he
Who does not see or know the difference.
Then: good and bad, higher and lower; blind is he
Who does not distinguish between the two levels,
And remembers the Real too late.
It is true that satan disguises himself; however:
The spirit, that unmasks him and burns the deceit,
Is so made that it can measure the whole world.

LXVIII

Simplicity and multiformity:
Two dimensions of All-Possibility;
Being is simple — Its qualities
Are without number, everything derives from them.

Or again: God is Unity, and the world
Is projected as multiplicity into nothingness.
All-Possibility means: to everyone his due —
What liberates thee is the Great One.

LXIX

The circle, the sphere, both are round;
Wherein lies the difference? Roundness is absolute —
No "more," no "less"; the sphere is not
More round than the circle, which contains everything.

Thus it is with the theory of Truth:
The theory is absolute, but it lacks
Gnosis, wisdom, sanctity; take care
That thy soul choose the Spirit — the whole.

LXX

In the beginning was the Logos. This means,
In the deepest sense: in the beginning was Being;
For God is pure "Yes" — no thing determines His Essence.
A "Yes" — thy heart should also be."

A "Yes" from out of the Divine. Let not thyself be enslaved
By psychic clutter; be thou the one to decide
What resounds within thee.
                          Prayer is free,
Because it avoids the delusion of the soul's desires.

LXXI

The line; then the cross that means four;
Then the cross that radiates as a triad;
And then the spiral that transforms the straight line
Into a rotating dynamic.

Then comes the static: firstly the point;
Then the triangle and the square; finally
The circle, primordial image of perfection,
Which brings to an end all play of lines.

All these are symbols that weave the universe,
And signs for the deep life of the spirit.

LXXII

Forgetfulness. The evil one often
Wants us to think of a thing
That is not worthwhile. God grant
That we only heed those things that are of use.

When we bear in mind the Highest Worth,
Then shall the path be free for other gifts.

LXXIII

Resignation to a void, to a not-being
For the Presence of the All —
Vacare Deo. Seemingly pure nothingness,
Paired with the Highest Fullness.

Be thou with God, pure of created things,
Then, in things, He will be with thee.

LXXIV

The prayer-wheels of the Himalayas —
It is not meaningless thus to turn one's prayers,
Nor to paint the *Mani* on stones,
Nor to have flags that flutter in the wind —

"May all beings be happy."
Thus spake Shakya-Muni. — Let the soul
Radiate all its power of benediction,
So that humanity will not be lacking in love.

LXXV

Two things are inexhaustible —
Firstly: the phenomena of this wide world;
Secondly: our relationship with the One,
With the Divinity, who holds the universe together.

Even if I gave up describing the world —
I could still speak endlessly of God and me.

LXXVI

I have told you much
About things of this world, great and small;
And much has the spirit composed, with God's help,
Concerning the path from nothingness to the All.

LXXVII

Hope and fear — contradictory feelings,
Which should not dominate our soul;
Being must be, God is the Highest Good;
In His Peace should our will repose —

Unconditionally. For we and the whole world
Are what God holds in His Hands.

LXXVIII

Vairagyānanda is a lofty name;
"The one who is blessed through equanimity of spirit" —
Behold how the Highest Truth confers peace,
Something the turmoil of the world never gives to the heart.

The *jivan-mukta*, to whom things are indifferent,
Is like the swan on a lotus-pond.

LXXIX

The pious must distinguish between two kinds of sin —
One is more outward, the other more inward;
The first sin violates a Scriptural law;
The second seeks pridefully to conquer God's Throne.

Either one violates a formal rule,
Or one sins against God's eternal Norm,
The weak human being can regret any sin;
Not every sin will the Most High forgive.

Remember that in Holy Scripture it is said:
The sin against the Holy Ghost will not be forgiven.

LXXX

Earth, Heaven, and hell; purgatory,
And transmigration. Do not rack
Your brain over these.
The good go to Heaven and the wicked go to hell.

You would like to know what no eye can see;
God knows best what will happen with you —
What lies in the destiny of creatures,
In Eternity. And that He knows, suffices.

LXXXI

The sage can understand what happens,
Not only because he is informed of the facts,
But also thanks to his insight into the nature of things,
Which pierces the wall of appearances.

For all things have their radiation,
And all kinds of criteria tell us
How things really are; thinking can often
Dispense with the what and the why.

LXXXII

Joseph in the Bible is an image
That is oft-repeated in history:
At first mistreated by his own people,
He finally sits in judgement over them.

The beginning of a reign has often been
A darkness of hatred and mockery;
Just as the thornbush, grey and misshapen,
Unfolds into the splendor of a rose.

LXXXIII

What does a child do who has a sense of grandeur?
Thou art a dreamer, his elders say.
The child can do nothing, but he can suffer —
He wishes to keep what for him is everything;

The great and the sacred are his dream.
Time passes, and life's green fades,
But the mature tree brings forth noble fruit —
Blessèd the man who has found himself in God.

LXXXIV

God is the Creator of the Universe. Therefore man,
His image, is an artist. Art is good in itself;
But since the nature of weak earthly man
Falters and degenerates, his art is often bad.

Art exists to rejoice the soul —
And above all to sow in our world seeds of the Divine.

LXXXV

Divinity; world, soul, Spirit. Domains which
All the branches of our wisdom teach us.
Firstly metaphysics, then cosmology;
And then psychological experience.
With *Sophia* blossoms the revelation
Of the most Inward — so let us honor the mystical life,

The Way to the True in the night of existence.
In the turmoil of the world, the heart had been lost;
In the realm of the mystical it was born anew —

God brought Selfhood to light.

LXXXVI

"If God did not exist, one would have to invent Him" —
So said a philosopher, otherwise not enlightened;
For sometimes a fool speaks a true word —
A fool, on whom ye have conferred the laurel of fame.

What is right with this idea is that God's Being
Is manifested not only by the religious form
And by the Intellect, but also — from without —
By human need; by the norm

Of the human state. Whoever will not believe in the Lord,
Belongs to the abnormal, the deaf.

LXXXVII

There is a space through which thou must pass;
It is thy destiny. Its narrow walls
Thou canst not break down. So see
If there is not another way out.

The way out exists, but it is upwards;
If thou findest it, thou mayst praise the Lord.
Will this be the end of destiny's space?
The answer is: yes and no.

LXXXVIII

The hero, the saint; what they meant for me
I had to hide from people;
The Truth was too profound, even if it were a dream —
My elders told me: dreams are like froth.

At school I lived among the Bible's palm trees —
With David's harp and his Psalms.
What I received there, I can hardly measure;
What I was given, I shall never forget.

LXXXIX

Shankara: That which is the stilling of all unrest,
In deep and self-forgetting Peace,
Wherein is neither loss nor gain —
That is Benares, that is what I am.

Who wove the *jīvan-mukta*'s soul?
Shankarāchārya was the lotus-chalice
That opens itself to the Light from Above.

XC

Al-Qutb — the "Pole" — he is called in Arabic,
And *Jagadguru* is the Sanskrit word:
"Master-Teacher for the whole earth" —
Not only for this or that place.
Ye may tend towards a narrow credo —
But the voice of the primordial age must be.
Who is this Master? Someone who can be named;
Or perhaps, if God so wills, someone unknown.

XCI

Plato's thinking tended Upwards,
            Aristotle's thinking tended towards the earth;
Similar is the relationship
            that we find between Shankara
And Ramanuja in India;
            both spiritual edifices
Had to be built,
            each one to shape a specific world.
Greece and India
            are not on the same level;
Hellas cannot be
            the *Sanātana Dharma*.

XCII

Man, as image of God, has something divine in him:
The Spirit, both sharply discerning and contemplative;
God made the soul's substance a servant —
But also a friend, wherefore we pray trustingly.

The soul fell into matter,
Through which we are burdened by our animal nature,
With all its joys and pains —

To God be the glory, we are only men.

XCIII

Earthly man is a knot of experience,
And these knots interact during life;
Wisdom is what can undo the knots —
One should not defenselessly cling to one's own ego.

Doubtless you have heard of the Gordian knot —
It was cleft by Alexander's sword.
And so it is with wisdom, for it can
Cut through the net of folly with one stroke.

XCIV

Truth and consciousness of Truth;
Or doctrine and way — an absolute with two aspects.
Likewise, beauty and love are
An absolute with two splendors.
Then the realm of virtue and greatness:
Humility before God and love of one's neighbor;
Might, with magnanimity, adorns the noble man —
For we are small in the face of the Most High.

XCV

The feet were made for moving forwards,
So it is with man: whoever plows, should not look back,
Otherwise the sowing is of no value. What lies before us
Is God; the last word of the good path is bliss.

Yet it is not enough to look ahead while walking —
The viaticum is trust in God.

XCVI

On a ship on the boundless sea —
India and Africa, from world to world;
The keel cuts boldly through the ocean
Beneath the limitless sky.

Such is the ego as it traverses the universe
On the path prescribed by the Most High.
The Self, Pure Being — the most profound conjunction —
But both are subject to the One.

XCVII

In Basel, where the red Cathedral stands,
The Rhine bends and flows towards the north —
And there it loses itself in the vast sea,
As if it wished to find its final rest.

Thus does the grace of illumination change the course
Of earthly life. Let us flow upwards,
Toward the spiritual North and the Eternal Sea —
And may God's Peace take us unto Itself.

XCVIII

Thou canst not prevent people
From having opinions; these cannot
Change Reality, nor darken
The God-given Light of the Pure Spirit.

Well, one can talk, though sometimes it is of no use —
The deaf will hear on Judgement Day.
God grant that they will understand what they should —
In the meantime, let them think what they will.

XCIX

Long live intelligence! You Sufis and *bhaktas*
Dream of love, and seem not to know
That love of God is also present in words;
That drunkenness is no soft cushion on which to rest;
That it is written: In the beginning was the Word;
That thought brings many blossoms to the heart;
And that the love-wine of doctrine
Is the nectar in which illusion vanishes.

C

Do not confuse pedantic reason,
Hair-splitting, endless vacillation
And brooding alien to the heart,
With thoughts given by God —

That lead you to the non-duality of Gnosis
And to the beatitudes of naked Truth.

CI

Certitude and Peace; then resignation
And trust in God. More we cannot want
Alongside the graces that Heaven bestows —
In the circle of duties that we must fulfill.

CII

Thou art my God, and I seek Thee
In hours light and dark.

Be still, my heart, and be not troubled —
For thy Lord hath found thee.

CIII

What is God-remembrance? Abstention
From any manifestation in the space of the soul;
Then pure activity, from God to God;
Then inward peace, far from earthly dream;
To understand that God is unique. Therefrom
Follows the awakening of thy Self —
To be united with Him, who always has been Unity.
Thus is completed the bouquet of the Spirit.

The human soul is healed in God.

CIV

A symbol is not only a sign, it is the thing itself:
It is an aspect of what it means;
In water, the humid element
Is profoundly united with what it signifies.
In fire, lies not only what thou seest,
It is the universal power of Wrath, that glows and burns.
God dwells in all the powers of Nature —
In every sign, revere the trace of God.

CV

O song of lute in a mild summer night —
Why dost thou come to mind, O sweetness?
I wish not to drive thee from the world,
Be what thou art. And I am what I am.

CVI

Ye sons of the desert! Why do ye stress
That God is One? Are there no other treasures
In the Divine? A thousandfold is the splendor
Of the All! But God is the One Protector.

CVII

The Highest Truth is a strong wine;
One would like to be at peace with all believers;
What the good-willed majority can grasp,
However weak it may be, one should let it live.
It is difficult to pour out all of wisdom —
One should not drown half-wisdom in wine.

CVIII

To be a human being would have no meaning,
Were there not the capacity to know and desire
That which is pure, invisible Reality —
The capacity to turn the soul from the animal to the Divine.

That a creature should love the Most High
Demonstrates why man exists.

CIX

Man's reason for existence is to be a mirror
Of the Real, the Divine. Nothing takes
Precedence over this; all things are ennobled
By the thought that loves the Most High.

In this thinking find thy rest —
Thy call to God is better than thyself.

CX

Thy Name, O Lord, is Presence of God —
And my invocation, before Thee,
Is my consciousness that Thou art near to me.

Grace makes the meeting deeper, dearer —
Because this encounter is Life,
It is the way to rise above our nothingness.

CXI

In principle, man is intelligent; he is not an animal.
But in fact, he is stupid — the proof:
Human history. If one seeks to understand it,
One understands nothing — one walks on ice.

We do not have the right to regret our humanity —
Because we have the choice to be truly man.

CXII

When I was a child, they wanted to make me
Something very fine: a lawyer,
A doctor or a chemist — a gentleman for whom
The whole city would have the highest esteem.

Yet, I envied the man
In a poor cobbler's shop, who, all day long,
Could think of whatever he wanted,
Free from all learned lumber, and wholly unhampered —

He could dream he was a yogi,
Free from all the delusion of society.

CXIII

My father was a violinist; he traveled
To Norway and Russia, and he taught me
Many things; and there was many a song
That would not leave my mind

And wove itself into the veil of my soul.
For the wise spirit loves the aura
That points the way to the blissful land of Beauty.

CXIV

My parents wanted me to be a painter;
But I read poets and wished to be like them,
And lived until my twelfth summer
In romanticism's somber melody.

Then came India, early enough; the poet
Still had his say, but never in the foreground;
Then he kept silent for many years.
                                        In old age
The poet awoke again — not in order to dream —
But to sing new songs sprung from the Spirit.

CXV

In life, something must happen,
Otherwise we could not call time life;
But there is God; and all that ever was
Is nothing, if we know it not in God.

In God-remembrance everything is near us,
The inward just as the outward. And so already
On earth, God willing, we are remote from time —
The Kingdom is nigh, Eternity is here.

CXVI

O mighty Time — let us see the Good,
And let what is not good vanish in the wind.
For thou bringest everything — certainly death,
And the judgement, and finally God.

But think not that thou art divine — be silent.
Thou hast power only because the Most High wills it.

CXVII

Evil is not a matter for wonder; it is here,
Thou see'st it every day; it is bad enough.
Look toward the good — it is wonderful,
And bears witness to the Creator, against all illusion.

In the good radiates the Absolute, the One,
Which cannot not be, and which vanquishes nothingness;
So be patient, and also grateful. Thou knowest
That everything lies in the hands of the Most High.

CXVIII

The wicked one desires two evils:
Despair, and lack of faith in the Absolute,
The great Invisible. Follow not the foolishness
Which summons thee in the garment of intelligence.

Right belief is salvation as such —
Believe first in God, and then in thyself.

CXIX

What coming from the enemy is a temptation,
Coming from God is a trial.
What the devil wants is a fall,
What the Lord wants is a deepening of the heart.

Thou, O man, who art every day in battle,
Underestimate not life's experience —
In the wake of absurdity and sorrow
Follows the revelation of the Spirit.

CXX

Existence is both being and nothingness —
The Lord has willed me, so I must will myself.
He is the Creator, so I must be creation;
I have no right to bear a grudge against being.

All-Possibility wishes to mirror Itself in souls —
Thou canst not close thy heart to love.

CXXI

His Name is emptiness, because of the
Vacare Deo. And emptiness is equivalent
To the Name; for where there is emptiness,
There is room for what benefits our heart.

The earth's fullness may — or may not — bear witness
To the Most High. It can contradict God
Or praise Him. Where there is emptiness,
Thou needst not break through a false fullness.

Where there is earthly fullness, there also is pain —
Not so in Pure Being. Be still, my heart.

CXXII

The All-Highest became, as it were, fullness
Through His creation; and creation,
For its part, had to become holy emptiness,
Through the God-willed call of the heart.

Ye are above delusion if ye know
That God's emptiness is the highest Fullness.

CXXIII

In every fullness there must also be emptiness;
The highest emptiness is the fullness of God.
For God's emptiness is pure "Yes" —
Self-affirmation is God's Will.

Before all creation, there was the One.

CXXIV

Blessèd are the poor in spirit;
The spiritual man is often called a child.
Whoever seeks to gain his life — will perish;
Whoever denies himself, is he who wins.

The world fades away — but the Truth remains.

CXXV

One would like to see the world in beauty;
But one must be resigned: the world
Is woven of oppositions:
The sublime is situated on the rim of nothingness.

CXXVI

Earthly consolation — it is allowed us
By Heaven, otherwise we could not live;
Yet our refuge must at all times
Be the Most High; otherwise we would not strive.

The Virgin spake: "They have no wine" —
For even the ascetic has the right to live.
Penance is made in order to save us —
But if it is bitter, it comes from the evil one.

CXXVII

Guardian angels are said to be good spirits
Who watch over us. Why do they not
Help us in every case? Firstly, because God
Wishes to try us; otherwise we would never learn the Good.
And then: stubbornness angers the spirit;
And so it too will close its door on us.

CXXVIII

Benares: where Hindus wish to die,
Because Ganga's water takes away all sin.
Therefore Shankara sings: I am Benares —
For his soul floats upon the waters;

His soul, free from burden, reposes in the True —
In *Ātmā*'s all-purifying flood.

CXXIX

Earth is the symbol of all fullness;
Air, water, fire, and ether are the emptiness
That purifies from the heaviness of existence.
To the Ganga river the honor of purity is due,
As to every symbol, that betokens the Most High.

Nothing purifies like Knowledge, the Light of God.

CXXX

The Presence of God in the form of woman
Is Laila — the Shaikh Al-'Alāwī could see her,
And speaks of her in a love-song;
His heart could understand the light of her beauty.

Woman, like music, is a Heavenly sign —
Made to transmit a word from God.

CXXXI

To be man is to dream; to be wise is to wake —
The wise man is a dreamer who awakes;
Who vanquishes his dream, who, with the grace
Of the Most High, shines in the night of existence —

And who, with a ray of Eternity,
Turns darkness into day.

CXXXII

Thou wishest to be logical, and indeed thou art;
But being realistic is also a part of it.
Thou canst not make the crooked world logical —
Think not that fools will leave thee in peace.
If everything happened as thou wouldst like,
This world would not be this world.

CXXXIII

Logic is one thing; quite other
Is psychology. But people replace
Clear thinking with psychological nonsense
That insults God's Being as well as our intellect.

They give precedence to ambiguity
And supposition, not to knowledge.

CXXXIV

Certainly man should think logically,
But above all he should think realistically!
When he sees things as they really are,
He can apply the laws of thought.

For a conclusion can only be right
If the point of departure is just and pure;
And so it is with man's soul, which only prospers
If its first step is consecrated to the True.

CXXXV

To err is human; firstly, because man
Does not know everything; and also because our senses can err.
We cannot understand why the stars
Rise and set, and we are confused
By many contradictions in Nature
And in ourselves.

Stubbornly to persevere in error,
When we know the Truth, comes from the evil one;
It is pride and bitterness.
God-created primordial man was not proud.

CXXXVI

Grieve not if thou hast thoughts
Thou wishest not to have; they are woven
Into the fabric of our soul, but far more often
They are whispered by the Enemy, to place on us burden
And pain. Say: God! and all is gone.

CXXXVII

Logic is not without value for the mind,
But intuition is the light of wisdom.
Cause and effect are meaningful for gnosis;
Syllogisms wisdom does not need.

Ātmā and *Māyā*: causality
Is the philosophical garment of Knowledge.

CXXXVIII

God calls us to account for the smallest things,
Yet His forgiveness knows no limits.
A contradiction? No, because the Lord erases
What we regret with a wise and noble heart —

No water purifies as thoroughly
As the knowledge that unites with God.

CXXXIX

Eckhart: a mortal sin thou shouldst not regret,
If thou canst now rejoice in the Grace of God. —
Here the Master speaks of Providence,
Not of sin as such.
                    May the Lord,
Who foresees everything, weave our destiny
Till the moment of Grace and all sin is forgiven.

CXL

God is the Weaver. Horizontal is the thread
Of necessary destiny; vertical the thread of graces —
Of the freedom that pierces destiny's tyranny;
God rules, but does not bind His Love.

CXLI

Existence, such as it must be, is mathematics;
Within it Mercy, which may be, is music.
If thou feelest at ease in the bonds of Truth,
Then God will also grant thee His grace.

CXLII

Regarding the Lord: there is anthropomorphism —
One thinks that God feels and acts like a man;
And then regarding God and man: there is voluntarism —
As if it were only a question of will.
Simple faith may be founded on this —
But it has nothing to do with pure Truth.

CXLIII

Islam teaches that the Koran
Should not be translated, for Arabic brings with it
Something of the Divine; and that it is of great value
That God's breath should enter our soul.

It is said that the Word became flesh,
And that the Buddhas deliver not only by their words,
But also by the language of their form;
So may God lend us of His Beauty.

The language of Revelation is a space
Through which the Holy Ghost has passed;
And may the man who drinks the sounds of Heaven,
Reach the Music of the Divine.

CXLIV

The right of the stronger exists in Nature;
Someone must survive, and it must be the better.
The law of earthly existence wills it so;
Yet there is not only the hard law of struggle —

To say struggle is to say generosity: for goodness
Is written into the nature of the noble warrior.
The strong man who has no sense of nobility —
He has remained in the realm of the beasts.

CXLV

Where Light shines, there stands also the traitor —
Judas, Abu Lahab, Devadatta.
But when the hero of Light appears in a dream,
Thou seest only him, and no evil-doer —
For if thou saw'st the latter it would not be true light,
But deceit. The evil one cannot
Show himself as good without betraying himself —
There is always a sign that unmasks the malefactor.

Mary has appeared multiple times, but never together
With a being from the evil one's realm.

CXLVI

The *Stella Matutina* is the star
Which, with its golden glow, promises a good day,
And, to the sailor who looks heavenwards,
Shows the right direction on the sea.

The Star of Truth: if thou hast awoken,
Thou wilt remember the Great One
Who is all, who enlightens and delivers thee;
God grant that He may shine within thy heart.

CXLVII

Meeting the Lord — it may be either effort
Or ease: act and hope or
Renunciation and peace. Whatever be my prayer,
I am the Lord's, and the Most High is mine.

CXLVIII

Firstly, discernment between *Ātmā* and *Māyā*;
Then concentration on *Ātmā* — often, indeed without ceasing.
These are the two poles of *Vedānta*;
They keep alive thy thinking and thy being.

Each one is the quintessence of the Love of God;
The religious denomination may be what it will —
As long as this double principle remain.

CXLIX

God is the Unconditioned. Then, through Him,
Comes the conditioned: the Prophet;
And then the pure Intellect within us — and also the Master;
God will forgive the one who honors all of these.

CL

Truth and Devotion. Truth is the light
That descends from God to Earth;
And Devotion is the incense, that rises
From us to the Highest Good.

Devotion — a sound, a wondrous word,
Fragrant with love and holy silence;
A magic word, whose beauty is enough
To convince us of the power of Truth.

The Most High knows what thy soul needs
Here below, where thou must conform to the world —
So be thou the incense that rises toward God.

CLI

Soul, dream not — be awake in the Sublime,
Who watches over everything. Dreaming is illusion
And leads to nothing. Waking is reality —
Therein are beauty and happiness enough.

Awake is thy heart in God. So be content
In the Lord; no greater Heaven hast thou here on earth.

CLII

Whoever, with faith and humility, calls on God,
Is saved. But whoever does so with doubt
Or leaves the Path, or tarnishes his calling
With pride, bitterness, or wrath —
He sins against the Holy Ghost;
Woe unto him, whose letter to Heaven the Lord tears up.

CLIII

Every word, even the best, can be twisted —
Woe unto him who misunderstands Truth and good advice,
Who interprets Wisdom as he pleases;
It is certain that his Path does not go upwards.

One would prefer always to speak mildly —
But one must think of the welfare of men.

CLIV

Twofold is the danger that befalls those
Who seek to serve God beyond their strength;
Either they lose their mind,
Or the Lord will be angry at their pride.

Pretenders, hypocrites — they are without number.
There are also good fools everywhere —
The fools of God — what can one do? One lets them be;
Faith will procure salvation for the fool.

CLV

In the forest where I dwell, lives the stag —
A holy animal, whose priestly antlers
Tend upwards like a king's crown;
To the stag the melody of legends bears witness.

The priest-king David sings in a psalm:
"As the hart panteth after the waterbrooks,
So panteth my soul after thee, O God" —

And so do I thirst for Thine Eternity.

CLVI

Initiation is a pact with God
With a view to the highest Reality: a promise
That the initiate be faithful unto death,
And betray not his word to the Most High —

His word to himself. God never says "no" to a soul,
Except when this soul itself chooses to break its word.

CLVII

Synthesis and analysis. Synthesis looks
Firmly at the essence of things;
The analytical mind looks with amazement
At the inexhaustible, and wonders if he can fathom it —
Just as a child looks at a Christmas tree.
For the synthetic mind, multiplicity is froth.

However: one must measure with both measures —
One must not forget the totality of the Spirit.

CLVIII

We are at the end of the twentieth century —
This age is indeed apocalyptic.
I do not wish to think of the unthinkable —
My heart dwells deep within Infinity.

CLIX

Purification. Thou wishest to be purified
Of all foolishness that distorts thy thinking;
And may God make our actions pure from illusion,
For all too often man loves what is false.

Yet foolishness can also lie in our acceptance
Of the illusion brewed by bad surroundings;
Mayst thou with a pure hand arrive at the goal —

With God's grace, which sees into our hearts.

CLX

The autumn wind blows through field and wood
Like a song accompanied by a lute.
I pleaded: O spring, come soon
As I gazed into the dusk.

Golden is the raiment of the trees
To beautify their death,
Toward the Kingdom of Eternity —
Everything sings of holy longing.

CLXI

Let us trust in God
Anew from day to day.
Here are Heaven's meadows
Where the Lord may bless us.

Here below, deeply in our hearts,
Resounds the song of love —
A song that was, before my life
Resounded in this world.

CLXII

A flock of birds flies towards the south —
For it is autumn. The birds glisten in the sun,
And soar aloft, rejoicing in the cool, pure air.
Their homeland has faded away.

So collect yourselves, ye souls; and blessèd be the heart
That finds its way to eternal summer.

CLXIII

Amongst the first words that I learnt
Were: "the Lord is my shepherd,"
And "I shall not want." — For a rich harvest
Is his who forgets world and I in God,
And overcomes all the deception of selfishness —

And finds himself anew in the Most High.

World Wheel

Second Collection

I

The world wheel turns as the Lord will —
Thou canst not stop it turning.
It carries thee along with it — thou wonderest whither;
God turns it also towards Heaven's heights.

II

Dialectic convinces us with ideas,
So that we may understand things abstractly;
Poetry has feeling, works with images
And seeks thereby to soften the austerity of thought —
So that we may see the truth with our heart.

III

"Veranda" comes from the Sanskrit word *waranda*:
The yogi loves to walk up and down,
Protected by walls and a roof — so that, when walking,
He sees nothing but his deepest Self.

IV

The wisdom and beauty of earthly things —
See how they teach us in different ways.
If we see in them God's intention,
Our spirit can find nourishment in their message,
And build many bridges to the Most High.

V

Discrimination is a different Way
From contemplation: the latter seeks
To live the True or the Essence — to be That which is —
Whereas the former wishes to perceive the nature of things,
So that the mind may know what God has willed.

What He has willed in the world around us
And in ourselves — what He loves in our heart.

VI

In China they say that wise men
Learn more from fools than fools
Learn from wise men. Only the wise
Have ears that to all things are open,

And can learn, not only from a "yes" or a "no,"
But also from the very being of things.

VII

In Paradise, what can one gaze upon?
Upon God; upon beauty, lotus trees and women.
In God's garden, there are no walls —
The inward and outward join hands.

VIII

Woman: since she is the incarnation of beauty,
Her body is the most beautiful thing that ye know.
Primordial woman is woven of two things:
She is a way either downwards or upwards;
A mystery of Divine Infinity —
A Path that leads fools astray and saves the wise.
And, as Dante said, in Heaven Eve sits at the feet of Mary —
In the same beatitude.

IX

When thou awakest, think not right away
Who and what thou art;
With thy first breath, remember
Who the Most High is.
On the basis of His Truth, thou seest then thy being
And the whole world —
Whatever thou thinkest and doest,
Should be submitted to Him.

X

Say not thy prayer has lasted too long,
For prayer is "now" — its time stands still.
No one, wherever he may be, is in a better state
Than he who mentions the Sovereign Good.
God-consciousness — in the most sacred Word —
Is far from duration, and has no abode.

Heaven does not abandon the weak —
An angel comes and softly prays for thee.

XI

Profane philosophers say
That one should think without presuppositions,
But this is impossible;
They fall into the trap of a skepticism that leads nowhere.
Not so the sage — deep within his heart speaks
The luminous and uncreated Truth of the Self.

XII

Synthesis and analysis — it is pointless to separate the two;
Everywhere thou needest both procedures.
Analysis reveals the structure of things;
Synthesis brings repose in knowledge and in life;
Outwardly and inwardly —
Thou canst conceive no better wisdom.
See how Pure Being divides Itself and becomes the world —
And how the illusion of multiplicity hurries back towards Unity.

XIII

I dreamt an unknown bard
Stood at my door
And sang, looking up at me
Unwaveringly.
He sang an ancient song of longing;
Its love-potion
Was heavy wine — as if he were
Sick at heart.

So may thy song stream, unceasing,
Over drunken chords —
Would that my grateful heart
Could accompany thy song,
And tell thee that morning is nigh.
The beauty of longing
Is indeed music; but deeper and sweeter
Are the sounds of Heaven.

Soon on the young horizon
The sun will appear —
Behold, all beauty's profundity is
In God's "yes.

XIV

In every son of man there are two souls:
One is created for time,
Where we wander in exile —
The other is for eternity.
It existed before we saw the light of the world —
God created it for the star-path of the Spirit.

XV

I was born on the Rhine, where it
Bends upwards, and flows towards the North Sea;
Now, in my old age, I live
In a forest, which shields me from the world.
The green Rhine is a symbol — it is the soul
Moving toward the Limitless;
And the forest: it is my final home —
The shelter on which God's Peace descends.

XVI

"He who goes to sea is not master of the wind."
A wise saying, and it seems to mean
That, whatever you undertake, you must do it in God's Name.
Remember well: you must bear the consequences.

XVII

I heard the gypsy's violin;
The melody
Was love-laden — he sang as though his heart
Would break in twain.

In the human heart is a kernel of suffering,
And yet it is sweet;
We feel what our soul has lost —
Paradise.

All suffering in life bears witness to this
Unconsciously;
But see: the consolation that God gives us dwells
Deep within our breast.

I wish, O gypsy, to be grateful to thee —
Much have I learned
From all the Beauty that thy playing
Brought to me.

XVIII

I have said it and will say it again:
There is certitude, and with it trust in God —
And there is peace of soul, serenity;
And ceaseless contemplation of the Lord in one's heart —

O one, O sole Beatitude!

XIX

The earth is a heavy, dark substance —
Into this mass man has fallen;
See how man's earthly instincts
Come together in a double play.

Man does indeed bring the Spirit into the world;
Yet his problem is not only this duty —
He dreams of salvation from earthly heaviness.
This is his existence — there is no other;

God grant that it be easy.

XX

Curious are the debates about medicine —
For or against homeopathy,
Or the treatments of Red Indian shamans,
Or the acupuncture of the Far-East,
Which heals by pricking nerve centers.

I never ask about mere theories —
Whatever helps, I call good medicine.

XXI

In our center, we have consciousness —
No better thing can a creature possess.
Pure Being is its highest content —
It is the crowning blessing of all God's gifts.
God gives Himself as liberating Truth,
And then, within ourselves, as Intellect and Bliss.

Thou hearest this in Eckhart's words:
In the soul, there is something beyond time;
Something uncreated — *et hoc est Intellectus.*

In *tasawwuf* it is said that the Sufi
Is not created; the Intellect proves this.
Both created and uncreated is the wise man's heart —
As is the kingdom of Heaven.

XXII

Port Vendres — here I had a dream-vision,
On the ship that was carrying me south;
It was in full daylight — my senses were not asleep —
The heavenly message approached clearly and sweetly

In a feminine form; as if she would say:
"I will take care of thee and thy preoccupations."
What could my soul expect after such a greeting?
It knew that it was in a heavenly garden.

True graces never vanish —
They help thee find thy true self.

XXIII

Do not blame people who wish to live only in the sands of the desert;
Do not exalt those who have a sense of earthly consolation —
On their path to God. May the Lord
Give us what His Wisdom has chosen for us.

XXIV

In his youth, Swami Ramdas was
A fine and earnest-looking ascetic;
When I met him, he was almost an old man —
And yet he was like a child out of a book.
How can one explain such a change?
Ram does not teach everyone in the same way —
Blessèd the man who goes to Heaven as a child.

XXV

Earthquakes must be, for the earth,
So heavy and powerful, cannot always be silent:
To living beings and to men, it must sometimes show
The primordial power of its profundity —
And God's wrath. Mountains that spew fire —
God wishes to lend the earth something of His power.

XXVI

A statesman was cowardly murdered —
He had the strength to shout: *Dios no muere!*
Strong words! To the doer his deed —
God dies not. To Him alone be the power and the glory.

XXVII

Kairós: the instant of all instants,
That brings good fortune and good choice;
Encounter with happiness, experience of God —
The now, of which the mystic speaks.

Kairós — the holy instant of the soul;
So choose it, that it also may choose thee.

XXVIII

At the forest fringe of my garden is a place
That pleased our friend Yellowtail;
Here he loved to stay in the sunshine
With us as brethren, taking part in the Indian life.
He is no longer of this world;
But the soul of the Red people is in the air —
And with it the Great Spirit, that never fades away.

XXIX

He who laughs last, laughs longest, says
A popular adage; it is a coarse saying, but true —
Yes, even full of wisdom. For the world's
Last word is the same as the first:
The word of the creation: Let there be Light!
And it came to pass.
                    And there is nothing better.

XXX

Truth and Presence — there is nothing greater;
Light and warmth permeate space.
God shines and vivifies. Thou art safe
In His Reality — the world is but a dream.

But even into it are woven light and warmth.
The omnipresence of the Lord — Him let us praise.

Truth, that bears witness to the Real —
And Presence, that inscribes the Real in our heart.

XXXI

The dim light of evening descended upon me —
O that the gentle sadness of soul
That old age musing brings with it
Could pass away like a shower of rain.

It passes away when God resounds in the heart.
Be still, O my soul, in thy silent night.
The sadness vanished. What didst thou think?
The All-Merciful thought of thee.

XXXII

Rabi'a 'Adawīya said: The question is
Not whether thou lovest the Most High,
But whether the Most High loves thee;
For this is what profits thy soul.

To things that are obvious, I say "yes,"
But not to an opinion that turns things upside-down.

XXXIII

Lalla Maghniah, a woman saint,
Dwelt in the mountains near the desert —
She lived naked before God's creative glance;
But from the *kadi*, she hid herself.

The body is not merely an earthly husk —
Yoga wills that it should radiate a blessing.

XXXIV

In life, one must make order from time to time —
There is so much paper to get rid of.
Where to put it? The soul needs fresh air —
One cannot always dream of the past.

See, every time has its own burden —
And, quick as lightning, think of God
And of life's meaning; herein there is no straying, no effort.

God comes to thee — thou hastenest to Him.

XXXV

Birthday — God the Creator decided
That I may enter into space and time:
That I may exist as a new human being;
Sprung from the realm of possibility —

A path of life, that gives a message,
And ends in the primordial source of all Truth.

XXXVI

I thank Thee, O God, for this breath —
It did me good.
It is Thy greeting out of the depth of my breast,
And gives me courage.
Ye know not the grace that lies in breathing —
It is nature,
Yet it is filled with God, with His presence —
It is not mere earth.

XXXVII

The German word *Atem*[1] comes from the Sanskrit *Ātmā*;
There are many deep meanings in everyday words.
In every breath, thou canst experience God —

I do not wish to expand on this as a philosopher,
For it is self-evident. We often speak without
Being touched by the deepest levels of language.

Language brings thoughts, ever anew —
Sometimes the words know more than we.

XXXVIII

One is almost ashamed to take pleasure in little things —
They gladden the soul, even though we know
That they are but trifles, and that we must nonetheless
Taste each day the earnestness of life.

Ye who are ashamed, do not forget
That even in little things, sparks of God's Presence appear.

XXXIX

Stand upon the ground
   The Lord has given thee —
Let not thyself be troubled
   By the outward or the inward.
Trials indeed must be,
   Both in the world and the soul —
Unshakable is God's ground,
   And steadfast His dwelling in the heart.

XL

Unconditional trust in God is difficult
And easy at the same time: difficult because unconditional;
And easy, because joy lies in its nature —
Just as thy destiny lies in God's Hands.

XLI

La vida es sueño[2] — of this there is no doubt;
But greater is the certainty of our being in God,
Of the duties that are sacred to us,
And of our return to the Great One.

XLII

With the saint there is, in a sense, more suffering —
And thus more patience — than with others;
He cannot clothe himself in easy lies —
He cannot wander through life without God;

Likewise, in holiness there is more happiness.
Be selfless — and do not look back on the naught.

XLIII

Hāfiz and Omar Khayyām were sages —
And also learned men; they drank from poetry's tankard,
Loving wine, woman, and song —
In the depth of the Spirit, and midst earthly illusion.

One could call "believing-unbelieving" those
Who know God's Light beyond form.

XLIV

I am indeed German, yet in certain respects
I feel Latin; the folk art of the German lands
Is foreign to me, for instance the tendency
Towards the ugly, fantastic, and grotesque —
Nightmarish romanticism has no appeal for me.

But in the German mentality, above all this haze,
There is intense feeling and tender imagination —
In music, fairy tales, and poetry.

A people should always keep a window open —
One can learn much from one's neighbor's gifts.

XLV

When Dante describes his *inferno* in a crude way,
It is not because he takes pleasure in somber imagery,
But because he feels obliged, as a poet,
To describe hell as it really is.

And also to describe Heaven, with Mary's splendor,
And Eve, Beatrice and Matilda —
Praise be to God, who made his final words so beautiful!

XLVI

One is often obliged to tire oneself with worldly things —
Be not afraid, for they will evaporate by themselves;
For God's Presence is always there —
So let it work in favor of the Spirit.
The law of life is the equilibrium
Between values, between "no" and "yes"—
Without this balance, there would be no existence.

XLVII

Why should man change as he becomes older?
For God remains God; the earth remains the same —
And so does man. What means the passage of time,
If we strive toward the kingdom of Heaven?

Old age — it is what life has taught us;
Blessèd the man who has honored the gifts of God.

XLVIII

Some craftsmanships we can scarcely understand:
For instance, wood-block carving. I choose my words with care:
Who has the time to carve so finely —
Even the smallest dot? To me it is incomprehensible.

The result may well enchant us;
That we cannot understand the process,
What does it matter? We must simply accept it.

XLIX

Doubtless, no one is omniscient. Consider this:
What thou canst not understand with thine intelligence,
What thou canst not make use of in thy path,
Thou shouldst readily lay aside.

And what pertains to the duty of thy function
Should not be a burden that disturbs thy peace.

L

Beauty of the Earth, and the language of its signs —
Thou canst, through these, reach many a deep meaning.

The performance of thy duty and the suffering of life —
Thou canst not avoid what God has ordained for thee.

God, and the radiance of His Face —
Be still, my heart, and do not grieve about anything.

LI

Space, time, form, number, matter:
These are the fundamental categories of sensorial existence.
Then ether, fire, air, water, earth:
These also are loaned by God to the world.
On the one hand, there are mass and energy;
On the other, there are life and consciousness,
And, above them all, Pure Spirit.
See how, in the limitless cosmos, everything that must be
Praises the Exalted Creator —
And how everything, born as it were of naught,
Circles round the one, uncreated Center.

LII

To whom belongs time, that passes so quickly?
To work, it is said, and I readily believe it.
And then? Blessèd the man who understands it aright:
The time that is there — it belongs to the Lord;

Even the time of work. Whatever thou doest —
Thy heart can always repose near the Most High.

LIII

What is the primordial substance of an object or a being?
Everything has three substances:
First, its mere existence; second, its species;
And third, whether it represents harmony
Or its contrary. Three times the same,
And yet different in the creation's kingdom.

LIV

In the realm of thought, the remembrance of God
Is objectivizing. In the heart,
It is unifying and subjectivizing. It is One,
In the distant other as in the profound "we";
The vision of God can be separative or unitive —

But all that I can be, I give to Thee.

LV

They love woman and wine, yet they are wise,
For they are Sufis. Living simultaneously
In the spheres of the world and the hereafter,
They can, while still on earth, hear the sounds of Heaven.

They live here, but towards the Inward —
For all beauty conveys profundity's meaning.

LVI

What is conversion? It is faith in the Word
In this or that form, depending on what we need.
One believes that, in a given ship, one can reach the haven of salvation,
And arrive in the Hands of God.

Conversion is also when disappointed in the world,
To finally turn to the thing that has meaning:
One feels that what is vain cannot be eternal —
One wishes to end in the presence of the Sovereign Good.

Conversion is to return
To what is our kernel — to honor God within ourselves.

LVII

Wrath, even when just, should not last —
For God is there, and thou must be there for Him.
Commend thy ways to Him with patience—
And let vexations go their way.

LVIII

In God's Presence, wrath should not persist —
Do not enclose thyself within thine indignation's walls.
However much an injustice annoys thee —
Above the clouds, the bright day shines.

LIX

One should not criticize the man of God —
For if he brings you wisdom from Heaven,
He cannot be an enemy of the Good;
God helps him, and the proof is that his spiritual work prospers.

In the ancient Orient, it never happened
That one passed judgment on the Master.

LX

Truth gives thinking objectivity and logic —
It means seeing things as they are;
From this comes also justice —
He who is truly humble, is not blind.

The eternal Truth shines into time.

LXI

For the remembrance of God there are guiding concepts —
Because thou must see God in all His splendor;
He is the One, yet also the All —
In the Name's mirror, thou shalt see Pure Being.

Beauty too is a guiding thought —
Blooming before the luminous heights of the Name.

LXII

It seems to me that something should happen —
Things cannot continue as they are.
There are people who are not intelligent enough,
And others who are all too clever.
Commit thy path unto the Lord,
So that He may bless what thou doest.

LXIII

The townsfolk wanted to have light in their little church —
So they let the sun shine into a sack,
And opened it in the dark building —
They knew not whether to laugh or weep.

The same happens in the real world —
Men do whatever enters their heads,
And wonder why, in spite of all their schemes,
Their world is upside-down.

LXIV

Remaining at the center should be thy virtue,
So that thou may'st blossom in eternal youth.
Flowing towards the Inward should be thy Path —
There is no better bridge to Heaven.

LXV

Thou see'st, O man, how the earthly world
Around thee crumbles into dust —

Happy the man whose heart has found the stream
That ultimately flows into the sea of Love.

LXVI

We love both freedom and safety —
The cool mountain height with its vast view,
And the cavern deep within the mountain —
The warm home, the happiness of a familiar hearth.

Both are symbols. Serenity;
And then beatitude in the depth of the heart.

LXVII

I think of the Real, and seek not to know more —
For anything I could know, is known to the Lord of the Worlds;
We learn many things, not because we wish to —
But only because we have to know them.

Certainly one has the right to think of many things —
But may God grant us discernment.

LXVIII

The human body, scientists say,
Represents what we need in order to live on this earth,
And nothing else. But it was not for this
That the Lord breathed into us the Holy Spirit.

The useful, in the structure of creatures,
Does not exhaust God's intention; for He created
Man for eternal life alone —
The wise soul follows the call of the Most High.

The human body is a multifaceted symbol —
Man and woman are complementary and yet one.

LXIX

One must admit that modern science
Blindly amasses the trivia of existence
Without knowing what things mean in depth —
That they can lead to the meaning of Pure Being.

LXX

To think of nothing has no spiritual value —
So might one suppose. But he who thinks nothing
Takes the trouble not without a serious reason —
He does so because this nothing leads to the True.
In God, the Void is a great Something —
Vacare Deo. To Pure Being be the glory!

LXXI

It is extremely painful when an innocent child,
Who from birth onwards only has goodwill,
Should cause disappointment. Why? It was not his fault —
Education paralyzed his genius.

Until he was freed from the chain that bound him —
Until he found himself through God's grace.
The child sought to dwell in the heights of the True —
His elders did not want this; they wanted him to be small —

They did not want a light to shine in the darkness.

LXXII

In India, it can happen that a woman
Of the highest caste reveals her breasts;
And that the natural sentiment of the people
Bows reverently before this nakedness.
Westerners, with prudence and piety, want
To cover what could be a temptation;
And, with decorum, to remain at ease.

Ask not, in this matter, what is God's will —
For God has willed more than one world.
Each one must follow the law of salvation —
You know how to act on your home ground.
Do what, in your land, is pleasing to God;
Not everyone was born on the banks of the Ganges —
And not everyone was born in Rome.

LXXIII

Goddesses of India: the blossoming of noble forms —
What is the meaning of the body's luxuriance?
That Truth wants Beauty, according to God's norms;
That Beauty is the splendor of the eternally True.

Only wisdom can exceed the beautiful:
First *Vedānta*, beyond space and time —
And then the drunkenness of dancing girls.

LXXIV

Nomadic Semites are iconoclasts;
Aryans and others are iconodules.
In an image made for worship, there can be benediction —
But it is dust; only God, the Spirit, will be victorious.

In Mecca, heathens had placed, along with other images,
An image of the Blessed Virgin on the walls of the Kaaba.
The Messenger of God could not bear the profanation —
But Mary he protected with his hands.

LXXV

Frithjof sought the hand of the king's daughter, Ingeborg;
The maiden's brothers saw in him an enemy and shame.
After many adventures, he finally came home;
He was victorious, and won wife, throne, and country.

It was the same with Joseph in the Bible:
Because of jealousy, his brothers hated and mistreated him;
He however became one of the great —
See how, in the end, he conquered, and forgave.

LXXVI

Herr Frithjof Thorsen was a ship's captain
In the storm-lashed fjords;
My father was his friend, whence my name —
A symbol from the distant, white North.

LXXVII

An injustice must not be allowed, just as the clock of life,
To persist in the stream of time;
Such would be a mockery of justice. Patience is ours,
Vengeance is God's — and the clock stands still.

LXXVIII

Outside by the city gate
I heard a minstrel's song —
A song that had resounded for years
In my inmost heart.

It sought to remind me
What my longing is —
An inward call from God:
The melody of the Eternal.

LXXIX

I hold fast to Thee, my God,
            and troubled will not be —
Let come what must,
            and let hope shine.
Whatever happens, God has willed,
            else it would not happen —
What does not lead thee to the Highest,
            is not written in God's book.

LXXX

The *Gaudeamus igitur* —
The stupidest thing I ever heard.
This is what was taught
To stupid boys at school.

To celebrate is certainly all right—
But one must know how;
Happy the one whose levity
God pardons in his final hour.

LXXXI

Truth offers more than the Beautiful;
But ecstasy is more than mere thinking —
Not, however, more than Truth. More than Truth
Neither earth nor Heaven can give.

LXXXII

If thou hast the Truth, thou must live from it —
Firstly in thinking, and secondly in doing.
Thy soul can repose in the Truth
Not only mentally, but also in action.

LXXXIII

Already in my earliest youth,
People came to me and emptied their hearts —
They felt help. It is the same today;
May the Lord illumine the house of my soul!

As a child, I knew not how it happened with me;
I heard myself speaking, and consolation was there.

LXXXIV

Sometimes one would like to enter into foreign lives,
And dream of fond, bygone places —
For instance, of Waldsee, in my grandfather's time —
Of dream-filled lanes, beneath old trees.

To re-live fading veils of the soul —
Be thou more faithful to the now of God-remembrance.

LXXXV

My late brother was a monk,
From his childhood a friend of the Red Indians.
Once a troupe of Red men came from across the sea;
He made firm friends of some of them.

He learned Lakota and, all his life,
He wrote letters in this language;
To his monastery Indians came several times —
He learned many wondrous Indian songs.

LXXXVI

In the sky above there is a doctrine:
Its deep blue is peace, but also fervor;
Sometimes the sky is white, and sometimes gold —
At every moment it bespeaks the Sovereign Good.

The sky, together with the sun and the rain,
Remind thee, when God wills, of His benediction;
Likewise at night: there is the sea of stars —
Infinity in the remoteness of the Supreme.

LXXXVII

Certitude — tell me: of what substance is it made?
It is something absolute — but with what right?
God's Truth itself conceived it —
In it, the least servant is king.

Certitude is Reality become Spirit —
Whoever possesses it, has gained Pure Being.

LXXXVIII

Mā shā'a 'Llāh: "As God wills."
Allāhu karīm: "God is generous."
These are the two pillars of Islam —
In God's Will, the soul becomes still.

LXXXIX

The efficacy of the essential is immediate;
What comes from the periphery, works only in an indirect manner —
If is based on earthly experience,
And benefits the spirit in a secondary way;
Yet any path to God is wonderful.

XC

There could well be a *darshan-yoga*:
Yoga through interiorizing contemplation.
Not only the sight of holy men deepens the soul,
But also the contemplation of beautiful women.

The form of the Buddha saves as does his doctrine —
So honor not only the Spirit, but also the body.

XCI

Everything in life could make us sad —
Why so? Because of the evanescence of things.
But be thou grateful and of good cheer, and stand
With one foot in Eternity.

Earthly existence can be what it will —
In the spiritual life, there is no time.

XCII

One day the great world wheel will stop.
Think not this is the end of all ends —
After each night there comes a new day.
The world wheel rests — then continues again.

XCIII

Powerful is the mechanism of this world —
However in one point joy shines through.
Not the joy of dispersion that is given by a toy —
But the beatitude of God's green meadow.

XCIV

Vengeance is mine, said the Lord. Nevertheless:
His also is the miracle — for to the Lord belong
Power and Goodness. And, instead of punishing,
He can convert many a heart.

XCV

Everyone wants to be unique and cannot be so —
This is the case of the Bible-religions.
If thou wishest the face of the One Truth,
Seek it in the islands where the gods dwell —

In loftiest and inmost realms.

XCVI

The soul cannot avoid scorn;
But hatred it should never carry within,
Except hatred of evil and sin;
What is diabolic, the Spirit should crush.

XCVII

The one that thou lovest must be worthy of it;
Others thou mayest put aside,
Or respect, according to their merit.
The one who loves everyone, is not capable of loving.

XCVIII

Thor was the god of wrath and storm;
Hence the name Thorsen, son of Thor.
The hammer, Mjölnir, was the god's weapon —
Thunder and lightning terrify everyone.
By his side was Freya: primordial femininity,
Goddess of mildness; beauty, love, and happiness —
Through her, wrath and strife flee back to naught.

All-Possibility: manifold is its light;
One can grasp it — yet one grasps it not.

XCIX

She was a *sannyāssini*, and would not live otherwise;
She wished everything to remind her of *Ātmā*'s radiation —
The Spirit and the body; and likewise the praise of God of the breasts,
Which, in breathing, move proudly up and down.

C

Everything that the Lord has apportioned to us
Bears witness to His creative power.
He is the Most High — remote within his Self;
Yet near in the wondrous splendor of His creation.

CI

What man receives from God, he should
Pass on to others; for it is more blessed
To give than to receive. So give, because God is He,
Whose noble giving is never exhausted.

CII

In space, pure existence is spherical:
Thus the sphere is the best image of Being,
And thus also an image of God's power —
This is the basics of cosmology.

From this comes the sphere's power to revolve,
To travel through space, to attract smaller objects —
For it wants to be strong, and *a priori* to live,
And in space to flee from nothingness.

The deepest dimension of physics proves
Why the earth goes round the sun.

CIII

The air is the bearer of light and warmth;
It is weightless like fire, not heavy like
Earth and water. It is the heavenly heights,
And also the storm, over land and sea.

Air is the breath that animates the world —
The incense-smoke that rises with our prayers,
And carries to Heaven our weal and woe.

CIV

Doctrine can suffice: there are men
Who need nothing more on the spiritual path;
But there are others, whose deepest nature requires
That they smoke the peace-pipe of Beauty.

For in the world of forms, there are many doors
Which, when properly opened, lead to the Truth.

CV

Thine acre is for thee a good field —
Be content that thy labor please the Lord.
Thou shouldst never scold other souls
Simply because they plow their own field.

CVI

Intelligence, character, and virtue — these three
Are everything, within God's Truth. Without it
Intelligence is worthless. Will-power and nobility —
They show us what, and how, we men should be.

CVII

Firstly, the Name, which is the whole Truth,
And which measures the values of earthly life;
Then resignation and trust —
May God build for thee the bridge.

CVIII

God hears thee — this is the message of the Supreme Name,
In which the human soul is born again
Through God's grace, and with the effort of the intellect;
The Supreme Name, in which the soul possesses everything and
    loses nothing.

CIX

The "Grace of state" — is freely given by God
To every guide of souls,
On condition that he possess genuine mastership;
With his benediction, you can strive upwards.

CX

Why did God fill the world with creatures?
In order to manifest Himself within the play of forms —
Just as a circle closes in on itself —
So as finally to repose in our spirit.

CXII

Strange is the profession of the actor —
He wishes to be a human being in all possible masks:
Hamlet, Macbeth, Othello; who am I?
Being nothing, I look deeply into the world —
O Self, thou revealest thyself in all.

CXIII

It is taught that only the One Self is real,
That the ego is but a reflected image.
In every creature, whatever be his nature,
Let us recognize the trace of the Great Self.
True, yet subtle — *Ātmā's* presence
Is only the invisible manifesting power;
Divinity does not radiate on our earthly level.

CXIV

All-Possibility: Oft have I spoken of thee;
Thou hast banished me to the dream of I-hood.
Such is the Self — It radiates through all souls;
As if It knew not which little ego to choose.

CXV

Comet-tail, in thy far-off splendor —
Thou didst exist when we did not yet exist.
Thou standest high in the sky's deep night —
Farewell for another thousand years!

CXVI

If thou hatest thy neighbor, God will hate thee;
Thou mayest kill him in open combat,
But not hate him. — Exercise justice.
Because God has created us for love.

CXVII

Thou wast born without wishing it;
Thou canst not blame the fates for their work.

What is life but a chain of images
That one would have liked to make more beautiful?

There are destinies that thou must simply endure —
And others that are thine own responsibility.

Natural instincts determine thee —
The one who is wise, overcomes himself.

CXVIII

One would like to hear the same thing a hundred times —
Why? To learn the Great One
Who gives meaning to all things. So let us repeat
One same Light — as do the stars.

CXIX

Trust in God is based on this thought:
God knows why He willed thine existence —
He knows thy gifts, thy needs,
And thy cares; and He knows how He should help.

CXX

Music, poetry, and visual beauty:
These accompany the light of Truth;
A daily bread for sensitive souls —
Not for mathematically-narrow minds;
Yet: they too should be able to grasp
That miracles of beauty bespeak the Most High.

CXXI

It may happen that the flow of thoughts
Suddenly hardens, as if turned to stone —
In opposition to what should be,
When the light of the Spirit reveals itself.

It is a play of nature — and it means
That too much thinking sometimes takes its revenge;
Man is made for the vision of God —
Through God's radiation, the soul becomes still.

CXXII

The brain becomes heavy, if it becomes its own goal —
If it forgets Being, and slips downwards;
But when the soul has reached its true goal,
It becomes like the wind — luminous and light.

Thou canst also observe the converse:
The weightiness of Truth can strengthen the soul.

"Only holy Silence brings me gain" —
Says Shankara in one of his hymns —
"This is the city of Benares, that I am."

CXXIII

I dreamt I was standing on a high place,
And could see all around the earth's rim.
I felt that God saw me from every side —
And I wanted, like a wheel, to turn towards God.

God is the Center. But at the same time He is
Omnipresence — the gaze from the kingdom of Heaven.

CXXIV

A man is everything that has happened to him —
He is also everything that he wished to accomplish,
And everything that was given him by God.
And every man — whatever, however and wherever he may be —
Must struggle with the world and with himself.

CXXV

Wisdom is more than human — this is true,
But man always remains man. He may struggle
In order to be more than a mere creature —
No wise man can jump over his ego.

It is true that the Pure Spirit is uncreated —
Aliquid increatum: Intellectus;
May God make thee conscious
Of what thou knowest in thy deepest heart.

CXXVI

Brahma Satyam; jagan mithyā; jivo
Brahmaiva nāparah. — In other words:
"Brahma is Reality; the world is appearance;
The soul is not different from Brahma."

There is no saying higher than this.

CXXVII

Thou shouldst love the Lord thy God with all thy strength —
And love thy neighbor as thyself.
Therein lie the law and the prophets —
This be inscribed in every human heart.

You may ask Jews and Christians about Wisdom:
It is the love of God, they will reply,
In accordance with what God has given them.

And if you ask the Moslem, he will tell you:
The highest good that God gave men
Is the truth that God is One —
The light of Wisdom that He bequeathed to the world.

CXXVIII

There is the doctrine, the Upanishad —
One can only understand it in the Pure Intellect;
And there are men who love Beauty —
And who, in its radiation, ripen towards *Ātmā*.

CXXIX

The Great Goddess is the Light of Wisdom, Sarasvatī;
She is also Durga, ephemerality,
The wheel of time that destroys the world;
And she is Lakshmī, blissfulness.

The Great Mahādevi is the universe —
Thou seest her not, but she is everywhere.

CXXX

The greatness of a man lies
In his relationship with absolute values —
And above all with Absolute Being.
This is what all the ancient sages taught.

It is miserable when a spiritual dwarf
Thinks himself an image of greatness; I would
Rather be honorable in a modest activity,
Than the stupid victim of undeserved honor.

CXXXI

Imagine that the world were thoroughly good —
Thou wouldst feel thyself to be in a heavenly garden,
And wouldst forget to struggle against thy foolishness,
To strive towards what is greater than thyself.
However, it takes all kinds to make a world —
In this way the Lord willed to ease the earthly deception.

All-Possibility: how often have I thought
That it did not make the world overly-good.

CXXXII

Whoever seeks to save himself, will lose himself before God;
Whoever seeks to lose himself for God —
The Creator and Measure of all things —
His works will draw him towards Heaven.

CXXXIII

The limitless bespeaks the Absolute;
The Absolute radiates Infinity;
God is Being, and as Being, He wills the world —
As world, He shines back to Eternity.

World Wheel

Third Collection

I

The world wheel turns, for it is time,
And it stands still when all times are silent —
To awaken again when God so wills,
At the proper hour — to Him belongs the universe's dance.

II

The Highest Reality I call Beyond-Being —
Then comes Creative Being: it radiates in all the things
To which it gives existence; If thou art wise,
Thou wilt hear the melody of the angels' wings.

III

Pythagoras — he brought the word of Wisdom,
So that the Spirit could find support in Truth;
And Plato, on the basis of the Eternal True,
Brought us the message of the Noble Beautiful —
So that, indirectly, it might lead us to Wisdom.
For God's House has more than one door.

IV

The *jagadguru* is an austere sage —
He deems the world not worth a button.
Quite other is the *tantra* master, who loves
To surround himself with a noble ring of beautiful women,
And with music. Neither should be criticized —
For every wise man will be ennobled by Heaven.

V

"Little Rose with the golden hair
Loved so much to dance;
She danced till it was evening,
And the moon and the stars were watching."

My father wrote these lines, and with them
There sang his noble violin;
He played, and his song was wine —
As the sun was sinking down.

The song floats in the evening air —
A longing for heavenly meadows.
If only the wounded heart could see
The Homeland already here below!

If only this song of longing
Could reveal its deepest core —
Beyond the heart's drunken dream,
The song of the Wonderful!

VI

O ye who have sound intellects,
Understand the doctrine that lies hidden
In the poem, which revolves like a wheel —

O voi ch'avete li'ntelletti sani,
Mirate la dottrina che s'asconde
Sotto 'l velame de li versi strani —

In the language of Dante. Often the poem's lines
Offer more than is contained in the literal wording —
Thou shouldst not simply dwell on the immediate meaning.

VII

Now, as I write, I am ninety years old;
See, how time passes.
Passes — what does this mean? Nothing to him
Who stands unshakably in the True.

For real is that we are with the Most High —
It is indifferent why time passes away.

VIII

I hold fast to Thee, my God,
And will know nothing else.
I believe in Thy Presence
And stand on firm ground.

"A mighty fortress is our God" —
This is well said.
Never has the evil one's ruse
Broken the strength of faith.

And if the Lord wishes to try me,
So be it; it will profit me;
I am not in my first night —
The morning will come soon.

IX

There is Krishna with his flute, whom
The circle of *gopis* venerate as the god of love;
And there is Krishna — both god and man —
Who in the Gita teaches the highest Wisdom.

X

Shri Abhinavagupta was surrounded
By *devadassis*, and with dance and music;
Shri Shankara on the other hand was an ascetic,
Who sought his happiness in solitude.

Two opposing poles within the Godhead's spheres —
And yet two human beings on this poor earth,
Oft difficult to understand — but nonetheless united
In One Truth, and at the same hearth.

XI

Man is intellect and strength; beauty and love
Are embodied and perfected in woman.
Both are human beings — may God grant
That the depths of their hearts remain divine.

XII

Wise men have for long told us
That the world is vanity.
Who can honestly say what it is?
If thou wilt not weep, then laugh.

XIII

The Divine is like a point;
Then, like a circle; and then, like empty space.
Unique; and All; Non-Duality, pure Unity.
God grant that this image may lead us to the True.

XIV

Naïve, brutal, and uncritical were the times
In which sanctity and wisdom blossomed;
One may well wonder why,
But must beware of false judgement.
The ancients always sensed the Absolute —
And readily saw good in the naïve.

XV

Whoever has a sense of absolute values,
Must know well the relative; one cannot separate appearance —
Which bears witness to the Most High —
From the Absolute Cause.
Cause and effect are closely linked —
The world is prefigured in the Godhead,
And conversely: we are penetrated by God.

XVI

"Be not troubled," said a voice to me;
And: "God is with thee."

"If there is a paradise on earth,
It is here, it is here, it is here."

XVII

Distraction; concentration: which gives us peace?
Concentration is the way of the spiritual powers;
And then distraction, so that thou become not tired,
For nature has its own rights —
Thou hast the right to be human here below.

Distraction is a way to something or other;
Concentration is the measure of God-Remembrance.

XVIII

The starting-point is what the Most High is;
Not some limited human faith.
Drink from the primordial source of the True —
Do not force the Truth under your narrow bonnet.

Not that I underestimate the various religious forms —
They too contain primordial wisdom in their sapiential depth.
Not to the husk, but to the spiritual core,
Is the highest honor due.

XIX

The *lā ilāha* is the negation of appearance;
The *illā 'Llāh* is the union of the intellect
With the Absolutely True, in the depths of the heart.
This means: the intellect soars above all things —
And in the heart, it manifests to thee the Most High.

XX

The *Avatāra*, founder of a religion,
Must have a veil around his vision,
Otherwise he could not found a particular form of faith —
For there are limits around the gifts of Heaven.

This applies to the outward, for the message
Cannot be everything. But inwardly,
And also on the plane of everyday logic,
The *Avatāra* is conscious of what matters.

Certainly not every rich man is an emperor —
But every *Avatāra* is a sage.

XXI

Amongst men of God, thou must
Distinguish three great levels: firstly the prophets;
Then the sages, founders of schools;
And then the pious men who pray best.

In this domain, no one is small;
Because it is greatness, in the midst of all miseries,
To be even the littlest Word of the Lord.

XXII

Megalomania is certainly a vice;
But paranoia is the cry of the evil one;
A delusion of grandeur is sometimes mere play —
Destructive madness is always satanic.
Protect thyself from both: do not overestimate thyself,
Remain far from blind passion;
For thy soul should stand in the presence of the Most High,
And never forget the nothingness of worldly illusion.

XXIII

There is something absolute in the soul —
Even in combat, thou shouldst not forget this.
On the one hand, thou hast the right to be human;
On the other hand, thou must measure with God's eternal measures.

XXIV

The rights of relativity
Are themselves relative; and the rights
Of the Absolute are themselves absolute —
One cannot fight over the light of the sun.

XXV

My grandmother loved to play her zither,
When she thought of her far-off youth;
Of the melody of days gone by —
Of a time when love still laughed.

If only she had known, free from pointless longing,
That youth is where we meet God:
Then the song of her zither would have been a prayer —

May God bless the discernment of the old.

XXVI

Prophets, like Abraham and Moses;
And sages, like Plato and Shankara;
Then saints — who can name them all?
These are the greatest the earth has seen.

XXVII

"Man proposes, God disposes" — a wise saying;
Should man limit himself to being patient?
He must indeed be man, what lesson should he draw?
His thinking and acting, he must offer to the Most High.

XXVIII

Beauty has degrees and styles; yet every
True beauty is perfect in itself.
Woman, as a human being, is the image of God;
But as woman, she ended manifestation;
For nothing can be more beautiful than pure beauty;
In her I see what I long for in my spirit.

Agar firdaus bar ruye zamīn ast,
Hamīn ast, u-hamīn ast, u-hamīn ast.
If there is a Paradise on earth, I say to thee,
It is here, it is here, it is here.

XXIX

What is the ego? All that happens to us,
And what we do, and what we see around us —
Yet, all this passes away like the wind.

As we stand before God, we are immortal.

XXX

Nel mezzo del cammin di nostra vita,
Mi ritrovai per una selva oscura:
"Midway along the path of life,
I found myself in a dark forest,"
As Dante said. When a trial approaches,
Be not concerned — God knows the seed of the Spirit.

XXXI

Esoterism: one can say everything,
But not everyone can bear it.
Beauty is esoteric: it enlightens
Only those who can see beyond worldly pleasure.
Beauty's path is holy — for it will show thee
How thy soul should ascend towards Heaven.

XXXII

A trial is the door to a new life;
Often a bitter crisis comes before a grace —
If there were no night, there would be no dawn.
Not easily does Isis show her body —
It is a ray of sunlight for all thy cares.

XXXIII

Folksongs — sometimes they come from poets,
Sometimes from the people alone, one knows not how;
Half soul and half spirit — earth and heaven;
The people's God-given melody.

XXXIV

"At the fountain in front of the gate" —
This is an old song.
I heard it in my childhood —
How swiftly time flies!

At the fountain — one wanted
To forget the bustle of the day's work,
And dream of fairy tales,
As if one were still a child.

XXXV

We find our happiness in God's will,
Accepting what He has ordained for us;
And then in the hope that He, when He wills,
Will grant our soul the ripe fruits of faith.

XXXVI

There are ideas that fascinate,
Such as the Real, consequently Unicity;
And then Union with the innermost Self —
Selfhood springs forth from the One Divine Being.

XXXVII

Truth is one thing; ambition is another;
Thou shouldst not mix the two.
If thou wishest to serve Truth, extinguish thyself —
The ego has no right to blur the meaning of Pure Being.

XXXVIII

I hold fast to God alone,
Everything will be better.
Truth and trust in God — there is
No better thing on earth.

XXXIX

Ye who feel certitude, beware:
Certitude can have different sources —
The criterion is its content, not its strength;
Only what comes from the Spirit is true and good.
Often what appears firm is but a vile deceit of the devil:
Stupidity and wickedness are the works of the evil one;
Better than this, is modest doubt.

XL

Of faithfulness my heart is made;
Unfaithfulness I cannot understand.
The dream of clouds is blown away —
The heart of the faithful does not fail.

XLI

If I were in Heaven, I would have joy in God —
Think not like this, for even in thine earthly garment,
Thou canst experience God's luminous presence;
Where there is faith, there is also joy.

XLII

Salām alaikum and *shalōm alēkhem* —
Heaven is peace; human history is strife.
Peace radiates from Pure Being
And destroys the folly of this world.
Unrest and vain triviality the evil one wants —
Peace was before the din of the world.

XLIII

"The vain chatter of philosophers" —
So said one, king among mystics.
I agree with the ancient philosophers;
A narrow mysticism means little to me —
And even less, a pointless quarrel.

Narrow-minded believers are not sinners,
They may be highly gifted, or like children;
I accept what they understand about God —
Provided they leave the others in peace.

XLIV

Fire and water: fire, a wild conflagration,
Yet also a motionless light before the altar;
Water, heavy and immobile in itself,
But also whipped up by a storm.
Behold the wondrous in these two elements: each power
Seeks to reproduce what characterizes the other.

XLV

That sense-perception is the source of wisdom,
Was doubtless, in Plato's mind, a ruse;
What is essential is the melody of the Ideas,
Whatever its way of entry into this world.

The Ideas are the Most High's possibilities;
Then the images of those possibilities, that we can conceive.
And only the contemplation and love of the Ideas
Can bestow on us Beatitude forever.

XLVI

Tell me what thou dost experience and how,
And I will tell thee who and what thou art — no more,
No less. Experience makes the man;
Before the Face of God, the ego does not count.

What then is the meaning of man, thou wilt ask?
That we carry something of God within our heart.

XLVII

Man is an accident, he could be another;
He is necessity, otherwise he would not exist.
Like an animal, he needs his daily bread;
Yet he is spirit — he bears the Light of the Most High.

XLVIII

She played the violin, and her only garment
Was her violin.
The strings sang, and the summer day
Came gently to an end.
She thought, the wine of music
Is not enough;
What, in art, one has to offer,
One must be.

XLIX

Form and color offer themselves to the eye;
A vast range of sounds offers itself to the ear.
All things have their meaning in the Inward —
Light and song impel us towards the heart.

L

The noble way to consider things,
Is always to take account of God's intention:
He created beauty as a path towards the inward,
Through which we can reach Eternal Beauty —
For those to whom this grace is granted.

So let us see, in the beautiful, the Presence of God,
And let vain things disappear into nothingness.

LI

Hold fast to the One, and thou wilt reach the One —
The True, which alone makes us happy,
Beyond erring ways, where we weep in vain —
Thou wilt reach the Light, where the heart rejoices in God.

Hold fast to the One, whose Grace will hold thee fast,
When in thy soul illusion falls away.

LII

It is difficult for me to understand why
A new day gives me something, and takes away something —
And why every day this ego becomes something new,
Constantly changing as it swims through existence.

Who am I, then? God, who gives life,
Is what I love, and it is He who loves me.

LIII

It has been said, that one should not
Allow what is personal to enter the spiritual life.
But one must rightly understand
What is one's own, and not for others.

The sage scarcely has a life of his own;
What he is in himself — he must freely give.

LIV

It is a fact that the next day
Does not always bring thee something better; so why have trust?
Because in the virtue of faith there are graces
That build for thee golden bridges for the better.

Faith can move mountains, it has been said —
Blessèd is he who has the courage to believe aright.

LV

Saints can be narrow and hard of heart —
What then is sanctity? Certainly, it is
Love of God, and nothing else; but man
Remains man within the orbit of his earthly tendencies.

The saint does not spare the land of the enemy;
Hence the wars of religion —
Even sainthood can strike the neighbor.

LVI

It may be disappointing, but it is true:
Saints were able to cruelly persecute
Those with beliefs other than their own. It would certainly be better
To seek more earnestly the Lord's forgiveness.

Certainly: to love God makes man better:
It gives him humility and goodness, and makes him honest —
But scarcely toward those with different beliefs.

The sage, faithful to the pure truth, could indicate
The right attitude — but he has to remain silent.

LVII

Is it not true that faith must fight
In order to protect one's spiritual heritage?
Certainly, but with due measure. To be pious does not mean
To cleave pious heads without consideration,
Or to oppress a harmless foreign people —
Instead of opposing the unjust amongst one's own.

LVIII

Concerning the right way of living,
Every saint is wise. And it is in the nature
Of wisdom that every sage is holy;
The Most High has chosen His own.

LIX

Wisdom in itself, and sanctity in itself —
They may, if God wills, remain hidden;
But sometimes these two miracles must shine —
God wishes to reveal them in the sunlight.

LX

One can often see strange contradictions
With highly gifted people: always in flight,
They are incredibly prolific and combine
Word-inebriation with profundity; hence Shakespeare's impact.
Actors may well live towards the outward —
But nonetheless can have their wisdom:
Besides playfulness, a sense of depth.
And doubtless the greatest poetic gifts.

LXI

The river of genius comes from man alone;
But — as with Dante — also from above:
The Creator has something to say to the world,
And the poet or artist has to carry the burden.
From both God and earth his work is woven.

LXII

Greatness in the arts is not always
A proof of greatness on the human plane;
The man may be small, but the value of his work
Is like an intervention of God in the world.
Greatness blossoms not only in the tracks of man —
God willing, it lies in nature itself.

LXIII

Against St. Anselm's thesis, it has been said
That this way of proving God is worthless;
That through it one could prove any absurdity,
Such as the darkness of sunlight.
A vain objection! Because: what counts
Is only That which is beyond the conditioned —
And not the desert sands of relativity.
Blessèd the man who, in the land of the Pure Spirit,
Measures with God's uncreated measures.

Something in the soul, says Eckhart,
Is uncreated: *Et hoc est Intellectus.*

LXIV

If someone tells you that tomorrow
Will be the last day in the history of the world —
You must nonetheless act as if the time
Until the Last Judgment were still a thousand years —

Thus spake the Prophet. And it was not a jest;
So take his wise saying to heart.

LXV

One could also say: if the last day
Will be tomorrow — or, on the contrary,
If thou still hast a hundred years to live:
This should be the same for thee — for thou standest before God;
Thou hast chosen the best, the eternal part in existence.

LXVI

There is serenity, and there is love:
The soaring above all earthly things,
And yet attachment to the belovèd —
And to God's graces that stream into the heart.

To soar, and yet to love — this is the song;
The song of everything that happens in God.

LXVII

Not every beautiful human being deserves love;
But beauty in itself deserves it —
I would that the heavenly ray of beauty
Were never attached to anyone unworthy of it.
But one cannot change the world. Between the two —
The earthly and the heavenly — one must discern.

LXVIII

"Ancient legends tell us
Of many wondrous things,
Of heroes highly praised,
And of great bravery."

The Song of the Nibelungen —
In the manner of the bards —
Contains the powerful myth
Of the setting sun.

Time, in its long journey,
Rushes and never stands still;
The solar hero, Siegfried —
He shines, but must pass away.

LXIX

The rising of the sun: God's messenger approaches;
The setting of the sun cannot disturb his victory;
The sun's orbit is God's shining yes —
After a short rest, Helios will return.

LXX

I know not who discovered the soap bubble —
Neither Copernicus nor Paracelsus,
Nor a philosopher brimful of ideas —
It must come from the fairy-tale land of children

And yet it is full of wisdom. For it shows
How a host of souls ascends to heaven,
Or how graces descend upon us,
Vivifying the earthly world with heavenly light;
And also how the soul, resplendent in its colors —
Each one unto itself — goes its own way.

LXXI

One cannot know all animals equally well;
Those I like best, I will mention here:
The lion, the tiger and the puma;
Also the little cat that often delights us;
And then the deer, the noble horse, the lama;
In the realm of birds, the eagle and the swan;
And the little birds that sing in the trees —
With this enumeration, let it suffice.

LXXII

The human type is one thing, its style of expression is another;
It is not always up to the level of the type.
So let us be patient —
What counts is that I see what God has willed.

LXXIII

Youthful beauty, finest adornment on earth,
Must change into beauty of age.
Values that were in the beauty of youth,
Must in old age reveal their mystery.

LXXIV

What is God-remembrance? It is impassibility
Within the din of the world, and trust in the Inward.
Serenity, certitude: thou shouldst remember them
Wherever, whenever, and however thou art.

LXXV

The first vision of God is birth —
This the wise man knows, but not the child.
The last meeting with God is death —
Blessèd are those who are in God's grace;

Those who, beyond time, found Heaven,
Because, in their hearts, they stood before the Most High.

LXXVI

If thou hast said that God is One,
Then thou hast said it all: for Unity
Is both Unicity and Selfhood;
Also Totality: the possibility of things.

Selfhood: the ego in its kernel
Touches the True Self, beyond time —
For God is nearness, despite remoteness and together with it.

LXXVII

Space is round; what is the meaning of roundness?
Firstly, perfection; and then, strange to say,
Childlikeness. Is not origin a child?
Femininity and goodness also lie therein.

And then comes time. What can one say of it?
It must carry the burden of coming and going —
Of change; time is the river, the strength,
With which God creates the destiny of forms.

LXXVIII

Ātmā and *Māyā*: the Absolute and the relative;
Cause and effect; man and woman; space and time;
Substance and mode; unity and with it totality —
Cosmic poles of the principial.

The primordial relationship, category —
First the thing, and then the where, when and how.

LXXIX

Let thy soul remain in silence for God —
May He fill it with His white wine:
White, because silence is innocence without garment;
Wine, because silence shines in beatitude.

LXXX

"A mighty fortress is our God"—
Always remember the Most High;
Forget Him not upon awakening —
And also remember thy neighbor.

The best thing thou canst give,
Is thy God-Remembrance —
Thou wilt, once the Lord has filled thee,
Give nothing better to the world.

LXXXI

It is said, out there in the world, that
Thou shouldst be useful to thy neighbor;
So tell him that he should
Always lean on the Most High.

LXXXII

Outside by the gate —
Why weepest thou? Dost thou not know
That God gives consolation
To him whose heart is breaking?

The consolation is not lost —
Ever remember this —
With it thou art born;
It belongs to thee eternally.

LXXXIII

In the morn of thy life's path,
Thou feelest fresh and free;
In the evening, when thou wish'st to continue,
All is already gone.

What life is, thou know'st not
When it lies ahead;
But thou know'st it all too well —
When God closes the door.

It may be that true life
Has not yet begun.
If thou livest in God, be it early or late,
Thou wilt attain the goal.

LXXXIV

A man of God in Spain saw the Blessed Virgin naked —
One could read of this only after his death.
This God-given vision of the highest, purest Beauty
Was the greatest day of his life.

They wish to canonize him. What he saw
Was the luminous archetype, the very heart of Mary;
This is what the Holy Scripture calls the First Wisdom —
It remains before God in Eternity.

LXXXV

Which is more vain: earthly things,
Or the people who overestimate them —
Who let themselves be lost in the snare of illusion,
And drive each other into the void?
Say not that I am an obdurate pessimist;
I merely see the world as it is —

But on the other hand, I see in it the beautiful,
For whose primal contents I yearn.
This world is not the land of eternal youth —
However: gratitude is a noble virtue.

LXXXVI

In the universe there is good and also evil;
The evil is mere privation, just a no;
The good is born of the yes alone;
And it is proof of a Supreme and Pure Being.

Were there no God, there could be no good;
Without a cause, the world could not exist.
Were thine essence not in the Highest Being,
Thou wouldst have no consciousness, no life.

To say existential form is to say contingency —
So leave the honor to necessity;
In the quintessence lies Reality.

LXXXVII

Inside a pyramid
Everything is black stone;
Thousands of years in darkness —
One is alone, alone.

Whereas in David's words:
Even if I were lost
In the deep valley of death —
Thou art with me, my Lord.

LXXXVIII

The last religion is founded on Unity,
On an Idea; this is what Islam brings us.
It is the message of the nature of things,
Which came to earth before the end.

To be wholly resigned to the Will of the One —
This is Islam; it has no other striving.

LXXXIX

Albertus Magnus: greatest of philosophers —
Synthesizing the thought of the ancient Greeks
And the Arab commentaries; sent
To give Christendom a rich spiritual treasury.

And Meister Eckhart: greatest of mystics,
Of a particular kind; totally focused
On the vision of God in the heart —
But independently of the traditional framework.

XC

Not without reason Virgil was Dante's guide;
For he was one of those rare sages
Who know everything in primordial nature —
Who praise God in His deepest mysteries,

And who, like Solomon — so often misunderstood —
Found, in the mysteries, the path to God.

XCI

Whatever happens around us —
One need not transform it into cares.
The soul should hold fast to God's Peace —
It is enough that we act in a reasonable way.

Remain in the still house of Wisdom,
And act from inward Being.

XCII

What is felicity? It is peace in the True:
God is real; the world is appearance;
The kernel of the soul is not other than God —
Hence felicity, the wine of the Spirit.

Hence also, out of the soul's holy kernel,
Humility and generosity. Beauty praises the Lord.

XCIII

Literalist believers, and the way of love;
Wise men, and the way of the knowledge of deepest causes.

Man chooses what chooses him, yet he is free —
As creation wishes, neither more nor less;
God grant that he may find the Truth.

XCIV

I believe in God, whom I have never seen;
But as a wise man, I know that He is there.
I know it, because I stand before Him;
And because I see Him in my heart.

What does it mean: I believe in Thee?
It must be so —Thou lookest on me.
So it is in the realm of the wise:
Faith and knowledge are the same.

In faith there is also this meaning:
With love, I strive towards Thee.

XCV

The known and the knower: two poles
In space and time. And therefrom comes a chain
Of possibilities: experience, which may or may not be;
May it be for thy good.

I and thou: and then God's Self in its Essence,
From the beginning, and until the final hour.

XCVI

World, life, people — these three concepts
Contain everything that destiny weaves;
Blessèd the man who sees through the stuff of existence,
And who in God rises above himself.

XCVII

The world, the ego. Doubtless there are people
Who always want to be conscious of their ego;
And others, who prefer to applaud this world
And its multi-colored illusion.

God and nothingness. And the spirit that knows both —
If it is conscious of the true Good,
Then, far from existential illusion,
It finds its joy in extinction before the Most High.

XCVIII

Life does not offer more than it can,
And if thou wishest more, thou must seek it afar;
Thou askest me what and where and how and when —
God will ordain for thee the portals of thy destiny.

Each must make his way through life —
At the same time, on a higher level, there is another way.

XCIX

Someone had the thought of pleasing me
By blowing soap bubbles in the air —
It was not idle play; the bubbles, which pass away,
Teach us, through an image, to see inner realities.

How was the origin of existence conceived?
It was made variegated, round, and colored.

C

Sat, Chit, and *Ananda*: Being, Consciousness,
And Bliss. So think not that the wise
Is sad because he knows so much —
His journey leads him to the joy of God.

CI

Ātmā is Reality, Pure Knowledge,
And Bliss. And thus God is
The One Who Is, the Seer, and Peace —
Thou canst name the Lord with a hundred names.

CII

What does the Vedic ternary *Sat-Chit-Ananda* mean?
Thou canst not separate bliss from truth.
The fruit of the highest knowledge is happiness of heart.
Whoever would live blissfully, must know Being and Spirit.

CIII

The ternary *Allāh, Rahmān, Rahīm* tells us
That God is One, and therefore also Totality;
Goodness in Itself, then radiation outwards —
That He does not forget the world of others, of the small.

CIV

Thou canst not know what thine ego will be
In later times; the ego is what happens to it,
Neither more nor less; and may God grant
That in thy soul, that which has meaning will conquer.

Someone who does not know where he will later stand,
Is nowhere. But long live his prayer!

CV

The sage knows why the poison of evil
Touches all creatures in the world.

It too is said: Verily, the splendor of My Goodness
Was in Pure Being before the power of My Wrath.

In our world: the necessity of evil —
One can, and cannot, resolve the enigma.

All-Possibility: who can grasp it aright?
We must let it be what it is.

CVI

Patience contains hope; hope needs patience;
After these days, other days will come.
In life, trials cannot not be —
Patience in God will receive its consolation.

I shall not want, for my Shepherd is there —
Happy the heart that has given itself to the Lord;
It will be given to graze by the Hand of the Most High.

CVII

The world is woven of possibilities:
Thou too must prepare thy loom.

Such is the world: the cup goes round —
Everyone has the draft of his future in his mouth.

On the other hand: man is free to choose —
Destiny cannot steal man's heart.

Life's picture is painted with duties;
Happy the man who pays his debt to God.

CVIII

There is the individual, there is society;
And then, in time, there is the generation
In which we live: a dream, and a web of dreams —
Yet a world that gives meaning to everything.

And within it, an instant, given by God,
Which — if grasped — enlightens and liberates.

CIX

How canst thou, O man, find peace of soul?
In the hour when thou thinkest of the Most High —
Of His Truth and of His Presence —
And givest scant attention to the ego and the world.

The hour of God is waiting at thy door —
But truer still: it is in thee, in thee.

CX

The sage holds in his hand the keys
For all possibilities, to see the ray of God —
To dominate the world's seductive play,
And to overcome the misery of all trials.

For one thing alone has weight in earthly life:
With God and in God, to soar above illusion.

CXI

If thou art tired of being with Shankara,
Then think of a beautiful woman — she will show thee
That the goddess Lakshmī does not disdain
To descend upon an earthly creature.

CXII

And if thou art tired of being in the world,
Remind thyself: God made the world;
For even in small things — within thyself —
Thou canst see something of God's wondrous splendor.

CXIII

Height and depth constitute the soul of the sage:
Height, because he soars above world and ego;
Depth, because, on the basis of certitude,
He lives the Presence of God in his heart.

CXIV

On the basis of certitude: *Brahma Satyam.*
If thou knowest this, thou canst know everything.
What thou knowest not, must not concern thee —
God knows it, and thou standest on firm ground.

CXV

In the war of religions, people did not know
How to fight and yet be generous with the enemy;
Neither side was wholly without justification:
For Luther, the sale of indulgences was evil;
Canisius wanted to abide in the House of Peter.
A pious, but nonetheless ambiguous struggle —
God will reward well the good intention.

CXVI

One should not always repeat the same thing —
But sometimes one is right to do so;
Heaven has often urged us
To openly accuse something that should not be.

One should not throw stones at the good,
Nor hasten to the aid of the wicked,
Nor add to the image of his evil character —
Nor should one reject anyone of good will.

Whoever flees the Grace of God cannot be healed.

CXVII

With Shakespeare, genius was in the foreground —
Then came wisdom. His energy for work
Was passionate and limitless: an urge to
Gather together everything human.

The poet listened to the call of Wisdom
That resounded from his soul and from Pure Being —
It was from that substance that he created worlds.

CXVIII

With Dante, poetic genius was the garment
Of his spirit, for which he lived and loved —
For which he produced his stream of poetry,
On a path often saddened by trials.

O voi, ch' avete li 'ntelleti sani:
Recognize the Truth that is hidden in these words;
Sotto 'l velame de li versi strani —
And that instills in the heart solace and salvation.

CXIX

To be a human being means to have consciousness.
But consciousness of what?
The essence of the Spirit is necessity,
Not chance. But in everyday life,
The content of our soul is mere possibility.

Consciousness of God: He alone must be.
And on this basis: consciousness of what is important;
And also legitimate play — sometimes at the same time;

The human state: a journey on a sword's edge.

CXX

Love poems, when deeply felt,
Are always a kind of love song to God.
Whoever truly loves, has found something divine —
In the midst of his earthly dream, he contemplates
The essence of love — and the Highest Good.

CXXI

Certitude of God, then certitude of salvation:
Truth, and faithful clinging to the Truth,
Bring certain salvation. What more wouldst thou know?
What thou knowest not, God knows; and it is for thy good.
Truth is the path to the wondrous.

CXXII

Everything that God made is a miracle;
And other miracles are woven into it,
Transcending the Law, but not Pure Being —
Existence is a never-ending stream from above.

Thou canst see God's Might in creation —
But His Might does not cease with the Initial Act.

CXXIII

Ask not why thou art here in the world,
Why God put thee in this place;
Thou art an instrument used by the Lord,
Into which He breathes His Holy Will.

God brings into the world that which must be —
Thou, O man, canst not be a mere accident.

CXXIV

Man is a thinking, inward being;
And also a being who acts; behold the world.
The Lord placed man before Himself, the Real, the Most High,
And then placed him in the vale of creation.

So think upon the Most High, the True Being,
And act in the sense of the True alone.

CXXV

God gave us reason and sentiment —
In the depths of our heart dwells the pure Spirit.
There is nothing in the wondrous structure of man
That does not of itself praise the Most High.

Reason was given thee by the Creator
In order that thou mayst live in the Real;
Beauty and love are the realm of sentiment.

The Spirit is uncreated intelligence.

CXXVI

In the North: cold, critical reason;
In the South: warm, loving sentiment.
The East: becoming and free creativity —
Imagination that looks toward the future;
The West: memory, that makes a synthesis,
And builds bridges from the past.

CXXVII

To learn: from Shankara, profound thinking;
From David, prayer that reaches God;
From Hōnen, faithful invocation —
The heart's urge to give itself to God, the All.
And Lallā: she traveled through the country
And danced naked, because she had found the Self.

CXXVIII

Learn from the song of the birds in the air,
From the sound of the wind in the forest, from the fragrance of flowers;
The languages God gave to nature,
May they rejoice and uplift thee —
Thou canst, O heart of man, learn from everything:
From the flowers by day, from the stars by night.

CXXIX

"The spirit is willing, but the flesh is weak" —
"Commit thy way unto the Lord, and He shall bring it to pass."
In life, there are labors, struggles, burdens:
Thou mayest well be weak — let God be thy strength.

CXXX

No doubt every person has some good traits of character —
But these traits are not always predominant;
Of what use is a touching and noble trait,
If insufficient in the picture of the soul?

Say not too hastily that an ordinary person is bad —
Nor that the first man thou seest is good.

CXXXI

It can happen that good women,
When in a bad mood, will concoct some stupidity;
Is this a privilege of feminine nature?
For this, only God knows the cure.

There are also irreproachable men
Who, though they know all the good rules,
Are nevertheless blind on certain points.
Why? Because human beings are human beings.

CXXXII

In the hereafter, it is said, we will meet again;
The heart's longing does not remain here below.
The Lord created us in order to love —
First in this world, and then in the better hereafter.

CXXXIII

One is tempted to regret the past —
In idle dreaming there is no profit.
What made thee sad, has cheated thee —
The most beautiful place is where I am with God.

CXXXIV

Esoterism is a two-edged sword —
It attracts both wise men and fools;
The vain seeker has not enough humility
To see that Wisdom is not a mania for mystery —
That wine is healthy, but for some destructive;
Only Wisdom that is well understood confers immortality.

CXXXV

The Presence of God is like a house —
"Blessèd be those who come in and go out";
Who move in the consciousness of God —
And place their souls in His hands.

God has invited us to salvation —
To us the merits, and from the Lord the graces.

Notes

1. *Atem* is the German word for "breath."
2. The title of the play by Calderón de la Barca, the Spanish dramatist of the 17th century.

Editor's Note: A few poems do not appear in this edition, but the original order and numbering have been retained.

Index of Foreign Quotations

Agar firdaus bar ruye zamīn ast, Hamīn ast, u-hamīn ast, u-hamīn ast (Persian): "If there is a Paradise on earth, it is here, it is here, it is here" (p.111).

Aliquid increatum: Intellectus (Latin): "Something uncreated: Intellect"; an abbreviated quotation from Meister Eckhart, the full form of which is: *aliquid est in anima quod est increatum et increabile; si tota anima esset talis, esset increata et increabilis; et hoc est Intellectus;* "there is something in the soul that is uncreated and uncreatable; if the whole soul were this, it would be uncreated and uncreatable; and this is the Intellect" (p.97).

Allāh, Rahmān, Rahīm (Arabic): "Allāh, Mercy, Compassion" (p.134).

Allāhu karīm (Arabic): "God is generous" (p.88).

Brahma Satyam (Sanskrit): "God is real" (p.138).

Brahma Satyam; jagan mithyā; jivo Brahmaiva nāparah (Sanskrit): "God is real, the world is appearance; the soul is like unto God" (p.98).

Dios no muere (Spanish): "God does not die" (p.68).

Et hoc est Intellectus (Latin): "And this is the Intellect" (pp.67, 121).

Gaudeamus igitur (Latin): "Let us therefore rejoice" (p.86).

In shā'a 'Llāh (Arabic): "If God wills" (p.16).

Lā ilāha illa 'Llāh (Arabic): "There is no divinity but God" (p.108).

La vida es sueño (Spanish): "Life is a dream" (p.73).

Mā shā'a 'Llāh (Arabic): "As God wills" (p.88).

Nel mezzo del cammin di nostra vita, / Mi ritrovai per una selva oscura (Italian): "Midway along the journey of our life I woke to find myself in a dark wood." From Dante's *Divina Commedia, Inferno I.* 1-2 (p.111).

O voi ch'avete li'ntelletti sani, / Mirate la dottrina che s'asconde / Sotto 'l velame de li versi strani (Italian): "Ye that have a healthy intellect, / Behold the doctrine that is hidden / beneath the veil of the strange verses." From Dante's *Divina Commedia, Inferno IX.* 61-63 (pp.104, 139).

Salām alaikum (Arabic): "Peace be with you" (p.114).

Sat-Chit-Ananda (Sanskrit): "Being-Consciousness-Bliss" (p.134).

Shalōm alēkhem (Hebrew): "Peace be with you" (p.114).

Stella Matutina (Latin): "The morning star" (p.49).

Vacare Deo (Latin): "To be empty in God" (pp.26, 41, 82).

Index of First Lines

Books by Frithjof Schuon

The Transcendent Unity of Religions
Spiritual Perspectives and Human Facts
Gnosis: Divine Wisdom
Language of the Self
Stations of Wisdom
Understanding Islam
Light on the Ancient Worlds
In the Tracks of Buddhism
Treasures of Buddhism
Logic and Transcendence
Esoterism as Principle and as Way
Castes and Races
Sufism: Veil and Quintessence
From the Divine to the Human
Christianity/Islam: Essays on Esoteric Ecumenicism
Survey of Metaphysics and Esoterism
In the Face of the Absolute
The Feathered Sun: Plains Indians in Art and Philosophy
To Have a Center
Roots of the Human Condition
Images of Primordial and Mystic Beauty: Paintings by Frithjof Schuon
Echoes of Perennial Wisdom
The Play of Masks
The Transfiguration of Man
The Eye of the Heart
Form and Substance in the Religions

Edited Writings of Frithjof Schuon

The Essential Writings of Frithjof Schuon, ed. Seyyed Hossein Nasr
The Fullness of God: Frithjof Schuon on Christianity,
ed. James S. Cutsinger
Prayer Fashions Man: Frithjof Schuon on the Spiritual Life,
ed. James S. Cutsinger
Art from the Sacred to the Profane: East and West
ed. Catherine Schuon

Poetry by Frithjof Schuon

Sulamith, Berna, Urs Graf Verlag, 1946

Tage- und Nächtebuch, Berna, Urs Graf Verlag, 1946

The Garland, Abodes, 1994

Road to the Heart: Poems, World Wisdom Books, 1995

Liebe, Verlag Herder Freiburg im Breisgau, 1997

Leben, Verlag Herder Freiburg im Breisgau, 1997

Glück, Verlag Herder Freiburg im Breisgau, 1997

Sinn, Verlag Herder Freiburg im Breisgau, 1997

Amor y Vida. Poesías, Mallorca, José J. de Olañeta, Editor, 1999

Sinngedigchte/Poésies didactiques, Volumes 1-10,
Sottens, Suisse, Editions Les Sept Flèches, 2000-2005

Songs for a Spiritual Traveler: Selected Poems, World Wisdom, 2001

Adastra & Stella Maris: Poems by Frithjof Schuon, World Wisdom, 2003

Autumn Leaves & The Ring: Poems by Frithjof Schuon, World Wisdom, 2007

Songs without Names: Volumes I-VI, World Wisdom, 2006

Songs without Names: Volumes VII-XII, World Wisdom, 2006

World Wheel: Volumes I-III, World Wisdom, 2006

World Wheel: Volumes IV-VII, World Wisdom, 2006